The Book of Proverbs
The Wisdom of Words

The Book of Proverbs
The Wisdom of Words

by

Michael A. Machado

PAULIST PRESS
New York/Mahwah, N.J.

Cover and interior design by Lynn Else
Interior art by Tim Machado

Library of Congress Cataloging-in-Publication Data

Machado, Michael A.
    The Book of Proverbs : the wisdom of words / by Michael A. Machado.
        p. cm.
    Includes bibliographcial references and index.
    ISBN 0-8091-4081-0
    1. Bible. O.T. Proverbs—Criticism, interpretation, etc. I. Title.

BS1465.2 .M33 2002
223'.706—dc21

                                                                2002007044

Published by Paulist Press
997 Macarthur Boulevard
Mahwah, New Jersey 07430

www.paulistpress.com

Printed and bound in the
United States of America

Contents

Contents

Contents

Dedication

To our three children, Mike, Tim, and Christine, this book has been dedicated as a father's legacy of love. It contains a tacit acknowledgement of the wisdom he has learned from them. This book is offered with the hope that, by following the counsels of wisdom, they in turn will lead a rich and fruitful life, allowing grace to build on nature and bring them closer to the fountain of wisdom, God himself.

And to those many other children who, someday as parent, teacher, or friend, hope to pass on their wisdom to succeeding generations, this book is dedicated.

Introductory Remarks

There is nothing original about this book, except its novel approach. It takes a fresh look at the appeal that the book of Proverbs has come to have. It shows how, for the most part, the sayings contained in it incessantly rise from the dust to clamor for our attention against those irreversible follies we commit in the course of a lifetime or, less frequently, how they energize our untapped resources for carrying out lofty achievements.

It imaginatively examines the origin, development, and usefulness of proverbs within the wisdom schools. It savors the best of what our collective humanity has to offer in the hope of reaching out for that "higher wisdom" that descends from above. It critically evaluates Proverbs' attitude to women, wealth, and the worrisome use of speech as pitfalls on the road to wisdom.

It attempts to give the readers an appreciation for proverbs as paradigms of literary excellence and as a veritable gold mine for speechwriters and speech makers, as well as all who wish to try out their literary skills.

Lastly, it highlights the drama of Dame Folly trying to parody Lady Wisdom in her bid to extend her clientele. In the end, she is revealed as a cheap imitation and an imposter. The curtain drops at the final triumph, when Lady Wisdom comes down from her exalted position only to find her second home in the faithful wife. After all, they both draw their inspiration from the same source: "The fear of the LORD," which is the beginning of wisdom.

This approach might seem a little too extravagant in the light of the historical-critical method. The latter looks for the minimum that can be stated. The language of appreciation revels in the hidden wealth it finds. If the attempt to look at proverbs as relevant for today is judged to be an embellishment of what the sages tried to do, then the author pleads guilty. Even so, he hopes that the readers, and especially his own children, for whom he first wrote this book, will find in it as much enjoyment as the author had in writing it.

Michael A. Machado
Professor Emeritus
Frostburg State University

Chapter 1

We All Love Proverbs, But Do We Really Need Wisdom?

Proverbs are delightfully witty. They are pleasing and provocative. But their real importance lies in being vehicles for communicating wisdom.

Sir Francis Bacon once said: "The genius, the wit and the spirit of a nation are discovered in its proverbs."[1] If what he said is true, that in itself would be a good enough reason for making the book of Proverbs one of the most interesting pieces of reading in the Bible. Aside from this, the book of Proverbs has a special interest of its own: the proverbs contained in it are presented as vehicles for communicating wisdom for successful living.

1. *We All Love Proverbs*

Why are proverbs so popular? There are many reasons:

Apt Descriptions of Situations. For one thing, we use them to advantage when they aptly describe the situation in which we find ourselves at any given moment. Sometimes, when my wife

1

Proverbs 11:22 *"Like a golden ring in a swine's snout is a beautiful woman with a rebellious disposition."*

is pressed for time, she might say to me: "Darling, will you please take this trash out and put it into the garbage can? And while you are about it, you might as well take all these groceries and put them in the storage room downstairs." So, to save myself time, I take all the trash in one hand and carry all the groceries in the other. As I make my way down the stairs, the trash bags slip out and fall all over the place. The vegetable cans and soft drinks fall out of the bags in a chaotic mess. At this critical point, she manages to throw one of her German proverbs at me: *Der faule Esel trägt sich auf einmal kaput* (The lazy donkey drags himself at one shot to his death). The aptness of the saying drives home the lesson.

A more classic example is the advice that Edgar Whitney used to give his pupils, eager to learn painting: "If you really want to be a painter, you must design like a turtle and paint like a rabbit."[2] It was his way of saying that the painting itself is not so important as the thought behind it. So one reason for the popularity of proverbs is that they provide apt illustrations for illuminating our understanding of a given situation.

Intrinsic Good Qualities. A second reason proverbs are popular is that they have intrinsic good qualities. They provide models of literary excellence, although much of their literary value is lost in translation.

They are short and easy to remember. How can one match the simplicity, terseness, and graphic beauty in contrast of Proverbs 14:13: "Even in laughter the heart may be sad, / and the end of joy may be sorrow"? In fact, in the ancient wisdom schools, the wisdom teacher required his pupils to commit to memory the wisdom sayings represented by the proverbs. This practice would serve a double advantage. It would teach the pupil skill in the art of writing (we shall have more to say about this later). It would also enable the pupil to enhance the quality of life by learning to apply the wisdom taught.

Wisdom sayings are not only short; they are also compact. In a few words they say much. For example, a simple statement such as: "He who keeps the precept keeps his life" (19:16) might make us curious to find out how. Proverbs contain deep layers of hidden meaning.[3] They tease us into making the costly effort to think them through in order to unravel their content. Their brevity calls for a certain discipline on the part of the pupil under the guidance of a skillful teacher. The word *discipline* and the expression *training in wise conduct* in Proverbs 1:2 and 3 refer to formal education. It is hard work; it requires diligent study, formal training, and arduous exercise or practice. The density that many proverbs carry would call for such a noble effort. For this reason alone, proverbs serve as sturdy competitors to lengthy, tedious arguments. In much of human discourse, it would be better to offer a proverb instead of an argument.

Besides being short and compact, proverbs are often expressed in picturesque language. They are seldom dull, but when expressed in striking imagery, they suddenly spring to life. Who can miss, for instance. the vivid imagery of the saying about a rebellious woman in Proverbs 11:22: "Like a golden ring in a swine's snout / is a beautiful woman with a rebellious disposition"? In Bedouin tribes, nose rings are seen as a sign of beauty. The point is that a rebellious spirit in a woman is as inappropriate as putting an ornament of beauty on a pig's snout. Despite their brevity, proverbs are complete in themselves. They arrest your attention. They are therefore easy to remember.

A fourth intrinsic quality of proverbs is that they are pointed. They are skillfully designed to drive home a point. They alert us to some definite action we need to take or folly we need to avoid. Never evasive or ambivalent, they go right through your soul and force you to a decision, course of action, or strategy. One who has never given thought to those less fortunate than oneself might be drawn to give heed to the counsel "He who has compassion on the poor lends to the LORD, / and he will repay him for his good deed" (19:17). Even a stingy character like Bogardis, in the movie

4

The Bells of St. Mary's, learns at last that a shining good deed toward the unfortunate can bring more lasting peace and happiness than all his wealth could give him.

Those wishing to improve their skill in writing or cultivate elegant, forceful, or eloquent speech would do well to pay attention to the form and structure of proverbs. Wisdom writers go to great trouble in attending to the skillful arrangement of the proverbs themselves. Certain forms, such as alliteration and assonance, are rarely, if ever, captured in translation. A good translator sometimes manages to pull it off beautifully as in the *Anchor Bible* version of Proverbs 13:20: "the fellow of fools will fare ill." Notice the alliteration in the words *fellow, fools, fare ill*. At the same time, listen to the sound of the letter *l* trickle over your tongue. We shall speak of special arrangements at a later time. For now, let us merely observe that the proverb's skillful arrangement sometimes made it possible for the wisdom teacher to recite one part, leaving the pupil to fill in the other part. For instance, the teacher might throw out the beginning of a sentence, such as "The toiler's appetite...," leaving the alert pupil to follow it with the words "...toils for him" (16:26 AB). That would make a neat alliteration with the letter *t*.

So proverbs are popular because we can use them to our advantage. They are handy little devices for getting our point across. Proverbs are also popular because of the attractive, intrinsic qualities they possess.

Universal Application. A third reason why proverbs are popular is the universality of their application. There are proverbs for almost every occasion and for different types of personalities. There are sayings for the just and the wicked, for the wise and the foolish, for the sluggard and the diligent. There are counsels pertaining to bribes, taking loans, making pledges, going to court, starting quarrels. Many counsels pertain to gossip, slander, detraction, and building good relationships. Proverbs cover a wide range of emotions, such as joy and sorrow, laughter and ridicule, anger and envy, pride and sloth, fear and remorse. Sometimes they put you at ease; at other times they churn your stomach. Sometimes they please and sometimes they tease. Some make you think on your feet and spring to action. Others may dismantle false expectations and cut you down to size. Some proverbs are like dangling carrots that get your adrenaline going. Or like Chinese fortune cookies, they turn up just the right message at the right time. Or they hit you with the impact of a *Reader's Digest* sweepstakes letter announcing that you may be the lucky winner and asking you to watch for the courier at your door with the first surprise check of $167,000 dollars. The universality of their appeal cuts across and transcends all barriers of race, nationality, time, and space. That is because proverbs go to the heart of something deeply human in all of us.

Truth Value. But the most enduring value of proverbs is that they express, in short, pithy sayings, something that common experience has shown to be true.[4] We cannot evade them because we cannot evade truth. They contain not abstract truth but, rather, practical wisdom. Or as Lord Russell would prefer to put it: a proverb contains "the wisdom of many and the wit of one."[5]

No wonder that proverbs enjoy a large measure of popularity. But why is such an important place given to wisdom? And why is wisdom literature, including the book of Proverbs, given a place among the inspired writings of the Bible? After all, much of what it has to say is secular in content and based, for the most part, on sheer common sense. Couldn't we just savor the proverb for its own sake without any thought or concern for wisdom? Is wisdom really so important, or even attainable? Do we really need wisdom?

2. Do We Really Need Wisdom?

The ancient people thought we did. As far back as the Sumerians more than two thousand years ago, and the Assyrians, the Babylonians, and the Egyptians who came after them, the collection of proverbs had been refined into a fine art. They laid out tried and tested ways of getting on in life and being successful. They held out the hope that, by imitating these models of wisdom, we too could gain access to the experiences of great men and women of the past (cf. 13:20). Originally these models were contained in folk sayings. When these sayings passed into common usage, they became proverbs. So, from earliest times, proverbs were used as devices for instilling wisdom.

Israel too had its own collection of folk sayings. Many of them were borrowed from other Eastern cultures, or they were reworded to fit Israel's own tradition. Even in the heyday of the priests and the prophets, the authority of the wisdom teacher was held to be equally paramount. In Jeremiah 18:18 all three avocations are put on the same footing. In this passage Jeremiah is seen as a troublemaker. His enemies are plotting to do away with him.

7

"Come," they say, "let us contrive a plot against Jeremiah. It will not mean the loss of instruction from the priests, nor of counsel from the wise, nor of messages from the prophets."

Priest, prophet, and sage have each their work cut out for them. One of the chief functions of the priest was to teach the Torah, God's sacred book of instruction. Prophets received a word from God along with the command to communicate that word to God's people. Both these offices received their inspiration from words directly or indirectly revealed by God. But the office of the sage was considered important in its own way. Its purpose was to pass on the ancestral wisdom of the past to future generations. Receiving God's word, incorporating that word into daily living, and living wisely all belong together.

Even the division of the Hebrew Bible into three parts: the Law (Torah), the Prophets, and the Writings, suggests that wise men and their writings were a kind of "third force." They complemented the ministry of the priest and the prophet. The third part, the Writings, is least dominated by priestly and prophetic interests. In it the wise man's counsel is most prominent. The authority to which the wisdom books appeal is the disciplined intelligence and moral experience of good men and women. God's word can do its work better in a nature that exhibits good judgment, sound, practical common sense, and a high degree of moral character. Grace builds on nature.

The wisdom lessons the ancient sages teach us are relevant even today. They serve as anchor points for guiding us in the art of successful living. Proverbs hold out the hope that we can come out ahead even in bad and difficult circumstances. They sometimes act as wake-up calls to deal effectively with the problem we are facing before it is too late. They put out stern reminders that actions often have consequences, that what we do often does affect others. Knowing the outcome beforehand can put us on guard against self-destructive behavior, just as surely as it can lead to fruitful, fulfilling, and meaningful existence. We can all be wise after the event. Proverbs teach us how to be wise before the event.

History is full of instances where wise persons often show up in critical situations. We find many such instances in the Old Testament writings.

Genesis 3 and Ezekiel 28:12–13 refer to a secret divine wisdom possessed by the archetypal man in "Eden, the garden of God." What our first parents possessed by a natural endowment we must struggle to attain.

The Joseph and Daniel narratives represent the Hebrew at a foreign court who was reputed for his wisdom. Their unique skills in interpreting dreams and signs baffled the professional men of Egypt and Babylon respectively.

Joseph is portrayed as the ideal wise man in his capacity as counselor and ruler (cf. Gen 37—47). He exhibits the kind of prudence, fidelity, and generosity that Proverbs holds up as distinctive marks of one who orders his life wisely (cf. Prov 10—25). His personal qualities of modesty, decorum, intelligence, goodness, and self-control are the very ones that the wisdom teacher tried to inculcate in his pupils as the moral prerequisites of wisdom. They are the very qualities that led a relatively unknown Hebrew boy to become the virtual ruler over Egypt. As Proverbs

18:16 states: "A man's gift [of wisdom] clears the way for him, / and gains him access to great men."

Daniel likewise showed exemplary courage and piety. The stories told about him, in the opening chapters of the book that bears his name, imply that his wisdom was of a higher order than that of the magicians and astrologers of Babylon.

Deuteronomy celebrates wisdom as the fruit of obedience to God's instruction (Torah). In 4:5–6, wisdom is seen as an acquired gift that comes from observing the Law. Joshua, who was handpicked to become Moses' successor, is a good illustration. Of Joshua it was said that he "was filled with the spirit of wisdom, since Moses had laid his hands upon him" (Deut 34:9).

Isaiah 28:23–29 adopts the style and thought of the wisdom teacher. Isaiah tells the parable of the farmer whose special skill "comes from the LORD of hosts; / wonderful is his counsel and great his wisdom" (28:29).

But wisdom was especially necessary for kings. Of all the kings of Israel, David enjoyed a special favor with God. He is described as a man after God's own heart. To David was ascribed wisdom like that of "an angel of God, so that he knows all things on earth" (2 Sam 14:20).

Solomon, David's son, became the legendary paragon of wisdom. His wisdom is said to have surpassed the wisdom of all the people of the east and the wisdom of Egypt (1 Kgs 5:10–12). The people of the east referred to in this passage are the people of the desert and of the desert fringe to the east and northeast of Palestine. Job is pictured as one of their great heroes (Job 1:1).

We All Love Proverbs, but Do We Really Need Wisdom?

Isaiah speaks of the future ideal king who would be a descendant of David. In Isaiah 11:1–2, we read, "The spirit of the LORD shall rest upon him: / a spirit of wisdom and of understanding, / A spirit of counsel and of strength, / a spirit of knowledge and of fear of the LORD."

All these examples go to show that wisdom was held in high esteem from as far back as we can remember. Wisdom teachers have always been in demand, especially in the ancient Mideastern cultures. Periodically, when people in the course of their history experience an upheaval, a hero invariably emerges who leads them out of their difficulties. The hero is then subsequently honored as a person of wisdom.

One such person in our own modern history is Benjamin Franklin. After the Revolutionary War, the delegates of the thirteen colonies sat down to draft a constitution. Matters came to a head when it reached the point where everyone objected to some part or other of the provisions. It looked as though the document would never be adopted. At this critical point, Benjamin Franklin, the elder statesman of the group, made an astute observation. Like the others, he did not agree with many of the provisions. Yet many times in his life he had changed his mind about his convictions and would most likely do so again. This might not be the best document in the world, but it was also far from being the worst, and he would certainly vote for it. It passed overwhelmingly. Franklin's good sense, discretion, and sound judgment earned him the reputation of being the "Father of American Wisdom."[6]

Such a timely, deft, and honest counsel as Benjamin Franklin's, emanating from his lived experience, can go a long way to make a seemingly hopeless situation bright and hopeful. By recognizing the wisdom of great men and women, we come one step closer to admiring and appreciating wisdom's source: God. Whenever our common humanity rises to its best, it is a sign that perhaps some portion of divine wisdom has become incarnate in us.

Chapter 2

Meet King Solomon
Did He Really Author the Proverbs Attributed to Him?

Solomon's spirit animates the wisdom of the proverbs even if he did not directly author them all. His example holds out a promise and a warning of how wisdom can be sought and found as well as squandered away or lost.

Proverbs 1:1 attributes the collection of sayings contained in it to King Solomon, son of David, king of Israel. Solomon was king from 961 to 922 B.C.E., and David ruled before him from 1000 to 961 B.C.E. Together their combined rule lasted nearly eighty years. Of these two kings, Solomon is remembered, even more than David, for his unique gift of wisdom.

Solomon's Reputation for Wisdom

At the commencement of his reign, Solomon asked for and received from God the gift of wisdom. We are told that God

Proverbs 18:16 *"A man's gift (of wisdom) clears the way for him, and gains him access to great men."*

gave Solomon "a heart so wise and understanding" that there never was any before or after him who could equal him in wisdom (1 Kgs 3:12; 5:10–12)

The precise nature of the wisdom he asked for and received was the ability to distinguish right from wrong and to administer justice (1 Kgs 3:9–12). This was illustrated in his judgment of the two women claiming the same baby (1 Kgs 3:16–28).

Solomon's wisdom is also displayed in his competence as a ruler. He succeeded in carving out an empire vaster than David's. It extended all the way to the Euphrates, to the borders of Egypt and Syria. With a genius for organization, he built up a whole administrative system of governance in which kings willingly gave him tribute in exchange for the security, prosperity, and peace they enjoyed. There was peace all over the empire (cf. Sir 47:13). Trade flourished. Profits swelled the coffers of the king's treasury. Gold and silver flowed in from every side. Even King Hiram of Tyre, a Phoenician city famed for its wisdom, paid Solomon a great compliment when he said: "Blessed be the LORD this day, who has given David a wise son to rule this numerous people" (1 Kgs 5:21). Proverbs may well be described as a picture storybook of the successful reign of King Solomon.

There is one description in which Solomon is reputed to have "uttered three thousand proverbs" and to have composed "a thousand and five" songs (1 Kgs 5:12). This statement is made in a context where the chronicler seems to lack words for extolling the utter magnificence of Solomon's kingdom: the vast extent of his dominion; the power of his chariot force; the incomparable splendor of his court; his wealth in silver and gold and exotic imports; his universal reputation, to which all peoples and kings paid tribute. The queen of Sheba traveled to Jerusalem to test Solomon's wisdom by asking him riddles (1 Kgs 10:1). We find examples of such teasing kinds of questions in the latter part of Proverbs (cf. 23:29). At the end of the arduous exercise in the battle of wits, the queen was forced to admit that the report she had heard about Solomon's wisdom was true (1 Kgs 10:6). Before departing, she told the servants how fortunate they were to be always in Solomon's presence and how privileged to hear his "wise sayings!" (1 Kgs 10:8; 2 Chr 9:7).

Lastly, Solomon seems to have mastered the classification lists of nature wisdom known as *onomastika* (1 Kgs 5:13). They concern sayings about trees, birds, animals, reptiles, and fish. Many proverbs that make allusion to such creatures may point to Solomon's influence. Despite these accomplishments, we still need to ask the question whether Solomon really authored the proverbs.

A Question of Authorship

First, contrary to what the title suggests, not all the proverbs attributed to Solomon were compiled by him. If they had been, it would have been unnecessary to designate two specific collections beginning at Proverbs 10:1 and 25:1 as coming from his pen.

Second, the two collections entitled "Sayings" and "Other Sayings of the Wise" (22:17—24:22 and 24:23–34) are based on an Egyptian work of the thirteenth century B.C.E. known as *The Instruction of Amen-em-ope.*[1]

Third, the second collection of Solomonic proverbs (beginning at Prov 25:1), we are told, was assembled by scribes under King Hezekiah some two centuries after King Solomon. Hezekiah was king of Judah from 715 to 688 B.C.E. According to 2 Chronicles 29—32, Hezekiah led a national revival with Solomon as his model. As the title in Proverbs 25:1 suggests, officials of King Hezekiah's court collected and edited proverbs that stemmed from the time of King Solomon. They were compiled either by King Solomon himself or by the royal schools founded by him. This explains why many of the proverbs repeat those in the earlier collection of Proverbs 10—22. Compare, for example, 27:12 and 22:3; 28:19 and 12:11; 29:3 and 10:1.

Fourth, two collections are ascribed to foreign kings: Agur (30:1–6) and Lemuel (31:1–9). They were presumably from Massa, in northern Arabia.

Fifth, many of the older collections were revised and edited to give them their present form by a wisdom teacher who composed the first nine chapters.[2] He lived sometime after the Babylonian exile about the fifth or fourth century B.C.E. So the final editing of the book of Proverbs must have taken place in the late Persian period (538–332 B.C.E.) or in the early Greek period (332–166 B.C.E.).

The title is therefore a statement of attribution, not a claim to authorship. So we may ask the question:

Why, Then, Is the Book of Proverbs Ascribed to King Solomon?

The answer is simple. In biblical times, it was not unusual to attribute material that had developed over many centuries to an esteemed figure of the past. Who better than King Solomon could fill this need? He seemed to be the logical choice because of his reputation for wisdom. We read in 1 Kings 5:11–12, "He was wiser than all other men." He also "uttered three thousand proverbs and his songs numbered a thousand and five." As one of Israel's most illustrious ancestors, Solomon's name would lend great authority to the sayings attributed to him.

But there is a deeper reason for the attribution. Solomon was responsible for introducing a wisdom school of teachers, based on the Egyptian model, and for the distinctive bilinear form of proverbs in the two collections associated with his name. There is ample evidence to suggest that a wisdom movement flourished at King Solomon's court and under his patronage. There is also evidence that his court was modeled on the Egyptian court, influenced by his principal wife (1 Kgs 3:1; 7:8) and by the state secretary (*soper*), who bore an Egyptian name (1 Kgs 4:3). It seems most likely that the major portion of Proverbs came largely out of the wisdom school founded by Solomon and under his direct patronage.

The records provide glimpses of scribes and sages at the royal courts of Kings David and Solomon (2 Sam 8:17; 20:25). As mentioned, one of the two scribes who held the office of king's secretary had an Egyptian name, and his son (Elihorep) served in the same capacity under King Solomon (1 Kgs 4:3). Such an official would keep records, read documents to the king (2 Kgs 22:8–10), and conduct the king's correspondence with other monarchs. He would have a staff of scribes working under him. One of their primary literary activities consisted in the beginnings of a consecutive narrative of Israel's past.[3] Since the scribe held a very important position in Egypt, as well as in the older Sumerian, Babylonian, and Assyrian cultures, it would be natural for Solomon to avail himself of a scribe's services. `

There was a second group of professional wise men who served as royal counselors (2 Sam 15:12, 31; 16:20, 23; 17:14). One of them would have the special title of the king's "friend" (2 Sam 15:37; 1 Kgs 4:5). Their counterparts would be available to offer their services to persons of lesser rank (2 Sam 14:2; 20:16–22; 1 Kgs 1:12).

The presence of scribes and sages at the royal court gives us a clue to the vigorous literary activity that must have been going on. There were chroniclers for detailing the narrative of Israel's past; record keepers to keep track of transactions between King Solomon and other royal personages; wisdom teachers to compile a curriculum of studies for training officials of the royal court. Scholars agree that the narrative of David's own reign and the story of Solomon's succession in 2 Samuel 9—20 and 1 Kings 1—2 is almost a contemporary account.

So also is the Joseph story, which came as a piece of "breaking news" about the time Solomon ascended the throne.[4] The story is contained in its broad outline in both the E and the J document. We know that the E document originated in the Northern Kingdom after the division of Solomon's kingdom. The fact that both documents report substantially the same story shows that the story came from a common source before the kingdom split into two.

In this story Joseph is portrayed as the ideal wise man. His wisdom is seen in his capacity as counselor and ruler. It is even more evident in his personal qualities of modesty, decorum, intelligence, virtue, and self-control. It is the saga of a man of humble beginnings who rose to the highest position at Pharaoh's court simply by reason of his wisdom. The portrait could have been drawn only by someone imbued with the views of the wisdom schools such as we find in Proverbs 10—29 and in the more ancient Egyptian "Instructions" (cf. Prov 1—9 and the wisdom sayings applying to kings in Prov 16 and Prov 22:29). The story found its echoes in the person of King Solomon himself, who embodied the wisdom spirit.

Solomon's influence pervades the entire structure of Proverbs, even though many portions of the book were being copied, refined, and edited during and after the reign of Solomon. Whether the wisdom sayings came from Solomon himself or from some of the wisdom teachers does not make a difference because Solomon embodied the wisdom spirit.

There is a moral in the ascription of Proverbs to King Solomon. So long as he remained faithful to God, everything seemed to go well. But when he betrayed God, wisdom miscarried. Solomon's kingdom was divided, and for many centuries there was no descendant of his on the throne. The efficacy of wordly wisdom, which most of Proverbs is about, is measured by the extent to which it is based on, and vindicated by, human experience. Only when human wisdom is brought in line with the first principle of wisdom, the "fear of the LORD," can it have lasting success.

Chapter 3

What Is Proverbs All About?
Content and Main Literary Genres

Proverbs were used as educational materials in the schools founded by King Solomon. They were part of the curriculum for wisdom teaching. They were designed for that purpose in their two main literary genres: (1) the instruction, an Egyptian import, and (2) the two-line poetic parallel form, presumed to be a creation of King Solomon or of the wisdom schools he founded.

The book of Proverbs contains instructional materials for teaching wisdom. These consist of wisdom sayings that are referred to in Hebrew as *mashal.* The root meaning of the word is a "comparison" or "likeness." The aim of the wisdom teacher is to find from experience the apt comparison, the right metaphor, or the suitable analogy with which to capture the lesson to be taught. Hence *mashal* may best be rendered as "paradigm" It contains a lesson to be learned, a model to imitate, a rule to follow But a *mashal* is always a work of art. It is a product of the poet's

Proverbs 4:1 *"Hear, O children, a father's instruction, be attentive, / that you may gain understanding!"*

skill and gains acceptance because of its pleasing use of language and imagery.

The chief device is, of course, the good comparison. For example, in order to describe the evil charms of an adulteress, the teacher may compare them to delicious sweets that later cause terrible stomachaches (5:3–4). Another popular tradition was to contrast the lazy person with the ant. How humiliating to think that even an ant is better than a lazy person (6:6–11)! So, in the gradual process of its development, a *mashal* comes to mean an authoritative utterance that carries great weight. It has the force of a moral injunction that should guide and regulate human conduct.

A *mashal* contains both an inspirational and a practical element. Its inspirational value is located in the source of the utterance. The immediate source is King Solomon, the paragon of wisdom. But it may even go beyond him to God, from whom Solomon received the gift of wisdom. In either case the utterance has the force of a divine oracle. For that reason the saying is profound and mysterious.

But a *mashal* has also a practical import. Its gravity is that of a moral injunction or maxim that needs to be carried out, executed, put into practice, even if it be at the risk of one's peril: "But the wicked will be cut off from the land, / the faithless will be rooted out of it" (2:22).

It is not enough that one tries to incorporate the offered wisdom purely on one's own initiative. One always needs help through the guidance of a wise teacher. Proverbs 1:5 provides the hermeneutical key to the entire work. The word for *guidance* in Hebrew means "steering." One needs to be led, guided, directed to take the right course. "The teaching is often enclosed in an expressed or hidden comparison which demands an effort of penetration necessary to grasp the meaning and import." [1]

Between the source and the recipient of the kingly art of wisdom stands the one who mediates this wisdom. Traditionally this would be the parent who exhorts the child or the teacher who instructs the pupil. But in Proverbs, this role is played by the wisdom teacher. He was a member of an elite literary circle, like the one who authored the Joseph story, or compiled the Solomonic and other proverbs and sayings, or edited the "instructions" in the first nine chapters. He would use literary devices for carefully crafting his message so as to make it more appealing. He would take great pains to refine his message until it had just the proper sound, rhythm, or structure. A play on word meanings, alliteration, assonance, parallelism—these were part of his trade.

The *mashal* carries a wide array of meanings. In biblical literature it can apply to a prophetic oracle (Isa 14:4); an allegory or a riddle (Ezek 16:2); a taunt (Deut 28:7); a solemn declaration (Job 27:1); a didactic poem (Ps 78:2); or proverbs couched in the form of poetic couplets (Prov 10—22 and 25—29). This last category makes up most of the book of Proverbs.

But the two main literary genres Proverbs uses for the purpose of teaching are the instruction and the proverb proper. The first nine chapters of the book of Proverbs concentrate mainly on the instruction mode. The remaining chapters rely on the proverb as a teaching tool as well as a learning device.

A brief definition of each will enable us to distinguish between these two classic approaches to learning. An *instruction* is "a poem in which a teacher or father is passing sage advice to his student or son." A *proverb*, on the other hand, is "a short pithy saying which expresses a truth learned from experience in a striking way."[2] The entire contents of the book are summed up in Proverbs 1:6: it contains proverbs (10—22; 25—29); parables (chs. 1—9); words of the wise (chs. 22—24); and riddles (chs. 30—31).

The proverbs, though mostly secular in tone and verifiable by human experience, ultimately receive their highest guarantee from the wisdom that comes from above. The guiding thread of the entire work is the motto "The fear of the LORD is the beginning of knowledge" (1:7). It occurs again in Proverbs 9:10 in an inverted form to serve as an inclusion at the beginning and end of the first nine chapters. It also occurs at the beginning, the middle, and the end of the whole book (1:7; 15:33; 31:30).[3]

This attempt to provide an inclusion for the first nine chapters, as well as for the work as a whole, is itself one of the many indicators that a later editor compiled the first nine chapters and put his finishing touches to the collections that eventually came to be what is now known as the book of Proverbs.

Chapter 4

Bring Out the Lesson Plan

Wisdom, the goal *of scribal education, is many-tiered. It includes being successful in life and, even more significant, being righteous before God. It is both a human endowment and a divine gift. How important, therefore, for the* instruction *to be carefully planned!*

When we review Proverbs 1:1–7 from the perspective of instructional materials, we clearly confront two things that teachers do. At the beginning of a lesson plan, they are required to write down a statement of the goal to be reached and the method for reaching that goal. In the wisdom schools, the goal of education is *wisdom*. The method and process for reaching this goal is *moral discipline* by way of instruction.

1. Statement of Goal

In a brisk opening sentence, Proverbs lays out the goal and the method of wisdom instruction: "That men may appreciate *wisdom* and *discipline*" (Prov 1:2). So we may ask: What is wis-

Proverbs 1:17 *"It is in vain that a net is spread before the eyes of any bird."*

dom *(hokmah)*? Immediately we are confronted with an array of word meanings, such as "learning," "intelligence," "righteousness," "resourcefulness," "knowledge," and "discretion." To the Hebrew consciousness, wisdom carries many layers of meaning.

(1) *Pragmatic.* At the most elementary level, *hokmah* refers to unusual skill or ability that results in making one an expert at a particular kind of task. It is acquired by training and experience. The secret of a true craftsman is the ability for designing and making objects of gold, silver, bronze, and so forth (cf. Bezalel in Exod 35:30–35 and Hiram of Tyre in 1 Kgs 7:13–14). Wisdom, in a pragmatic sense, is the right way to make or do things. And so we hear of the "wisdom" of warriors, sailors, farmers, and soothsayers, as well as of scribes, priests, counselors, judges, and kings.

But *hokmah* was particularly necessary for kings, such as David, to whom was ascribed wisdom like that of "an angel of God, so that he knows all things on earth" (2 Sam 14:20). Solomon was considered to be the embodiment of wisdom and its most excellent example. Isaiah described his ideal king as one upon whom "the spirit of the LORD shall rest.../ a spirit of wisdom and of understanding, / a spirit of counsel and of strength, / a spirit of knowledge and of fear of the LORD" (Isa 11:2).

(2) *Experiential.* A second level of meaning is skill in living. It is the ability, whether natural or acquired, for getting on in life, for being successful. Abilities like shrewd observation, sound judgment, and common sense enable us to manage our affairs, run a household, build a good marriage, make profitable deals, maintain good relations. Here wisdom is seen from an experiential point of view.

(3) *Moral.* At a higher level, wisdom is defined in terms of moral righteousness. Proverbs 1:3 speaks of it as "training in wise conduct, / in what is right, just and honest." When good moral conduct undergirds our attempts at being successful, it enhances our trustworthiness, our dependability. It gives more stability and staying power to our life. It takes a great deal of discernment, discretion, resourcefulness, and understanding to make the right moral choices. In this sense, wisdom is simply the ability to do what is right. It has to do with order in a well-ordered universe. We reproduce in our lives the order we discern in the universe (cf. Ps 19).

(4) *Philosophical.* At a fourth, or philosophical, level, wisdom consists in the ability to find meaning in existence despite the

ultimate uncertainties of life, such as sickness, suffering, reversal of fortunes, catastrophic upheavals, and death. We may find ourselves unable to reverse these "limit situations," but wisdom can always get around them by finding meaning and purpose within the constraints imposed on us. An illustration of this kind of wisdom is found in Job, but it is not found in Proverbs.

(5) *Spiritual.* The highest level of wisdom consists in letting God tell us, teach us, and guide us in what we are to do. We recognize that our capacity to grasp wisdom is limited.[1] Despite all our natural gifts and endowments, we come to a point where we lack the wisdom we seek. Only God can confer it on us as a gift because wisdom is an attribute of God. It belongs to the very nature of God. It is given freely to those who earnestly seek God, as Solomon and David did, who make God their ally by following God's commandments and living in covenant relation with God.

Both Isaiah and Jeremiah exemplify this kind of wisdom. They received word from God that the alliance with Egypt, which the king's counselors strongly advised, would be a costly mistake (cf. Isa 20 and Jer 2:18, 36; 37:7). They proved to be right. Judah suffered a severe defeat at the hands of its enemies. To the king's counselors, what seemed to be the good and wise and proper thing to do was in fact sheer folly. The man or woman of God can sometimes come by a wisdom that is hidden from others. Wisdom is a graced perception of what God has ordained will happen and the ability to act accordingly. A description of "higher" wisdom's blessings is detailed in Proverbs 2:1–22. The guidance that comes to us from living in covenant relation with God is this higher wisdom.

Keeping in mind the different layers of meaning that wisdom carries, we can arrive at a simple definition: wisdom is practical knowledge that when applied makes for successful living. We come by such knowledge through trial and error in the daily course of events. Sometimes it comes to us as a premonition, sometimes as a gift from God. Even then it needs to be tested and found true before it becomes stored in our experience as practical wisdom.

Secular wisdom—getting on in life, being successful, improving the quality of life—is the goal of proverbial teaching. Its standpoint is midway between that of the book of Job and that of Sirach. In the one, wisdom is ultimately a divine secret (Job 28:12, 20, 23). In the other, wisdom is said to be revealed in the law of Moses (Sir 24:1–12, 22). It is enhanced, becomes brighter and more beautiful when it fits in with God's divinely ordained plan for us. This implies an ongoing obedience to God's word and an ongoing covenant relationship with him. That is why, in the final analysis, "the fear of the LORD is the beginning of knowledge" (1:7).

2. Method and Process: *The Instructional Mode of Teaching Wisdom*

In the Egyptian tradition, the "instruction" is framed as the address of a father to his son or, since this is really a metaphor, from a teacher to a pupil. This is in recognition of the fact that the earliest, and still the primary, form of schooling was done in the home. Proverbs 4:1–4 reminds us of this sobering thought: "Hear, O children, a father's instruction, / be attentive, that you may gain understanding! / Yes, excellent advice I give you; / my teaching do not forsake. / When I was my father's child, / frail, yet the darling of my mother, / He taught me, and said to me: / "Let your heart hold fast my words: / keep my commands, that you may live!" Traditional wisdom sayings were administered by the father, and sometimes also by the mother. As occasion arose, the parents would pass on sage advice to their children. The advice was practical in nature and was given in a spontaneous manner.

As Israel emerged from its tribal past, the instruction was continued in the school in a more formal setting. Solomon carried this method of instruction one step further. He instituted wisdom schools, based on the Egyptian model, for instructing officials of the royal court in the art and practice of wisdom. While the Egyptian model of instruction clearly requires a school setting, the same is not true for Israel's instruction. Even though Hebrew wisdom instruction is appropriate for a school setting and an upper-class audience, it is equally suited to a family setting and a wider, less privileged audience. The opening verses seem to suggest that Proverbs was compiled as a practical guide for teaching wisdom in the home.

3. Sample of a Lesson Plan (1:8–19)

The "instruction" model is a carefully articulated educational tool. It has a set arrangement that makes it easy to appropriate the lesson taught. There are four distinct parts, although some of these may overlap at times.

(1) First, there is *a summons to listen*. The teacher issues a call to attention:

> Hear, my son, your father's instruction,
> and reject not your mother's teaching; (1:8)[2]

The best possible environment that the teacher can create is one that effectively catches the pupils' attention. Once they are disposed to listen, the rest will follow smoothly. There is a subtle power in that simple word "Hear" *(Shema)*! But when it is uttered with the loving authority of a parent, its power for engaging the full attention of the pupil is enhanced.

(2) Second, the wisdom teacher offers some *motivation* for carrying out his instruction:

> A graceful diadem will they be for your head;
> a torque for your neck. (1:9)

A headdress is a symbol of authority and honor. A necklace, usually made of silver or coral beads, serves as an ornament that gives the wearer an air of distinction. The point is well made: wisdom will sit well on the recipient. It will make him stand out and be respected by all who hear him speak. It will set him apart from all the others in society.

In the comparison between wisdom and the ornaments of dress, there is perhaps a subtle hint that we may be witnessing an address at a graduation ceremony. The lesson has in view young men who are about to go out into the world, their training behind them. Hopefully, in their newfound freedom, the moral principles that have been inculcated in them will be their safeguard.

(3) Third, the wisdom teacher proceeds to give *admonitions* on what to do and what to avoid. The motivation for carrying them out is already in place. The teacher must now get his message

across. For the beginner in wisdom, the most important lesson is to recognize how easily one can be seduced into doing evil for reasons of personal gain. So the teacher paints a vivid picture of a crime in the making. He gives a thumbnail sketch of a general life of crime and extortion that promises to be financially rewarding. The pupil must be made to see that crime does not pay. So this is what the teacher admonishes the unwary young pupils to do:

> Walk not in the way with them,
> hold back your foot from their path! (1:15)

He paints a vivid picture of a life of organized crime into which they are being seduced. They would be an easy catch for professional crime peddlers He shows them the temptation of shared profits dangling like carrots before their eyes. He warns them to "stop! hold back!" before it is too late. But what is his strategy for deterrence? For this, we must proceed to the most important part of the instruction.

(4) And so, fourth, he must point out to them *the consequences of their actions,* good or bad. By giving them a preview of where they are heading, he hopes to stop them in the tracks:

> [For their feet run to evil,
> they hasten to shed blood.] (1:16)

Verse 17 clinches the argument:

> It is in vain that a net is spread
> before the eyes of any bird—(1:17)

The proverb has a stinging effect. Birds are so naive that they easily walk into a trap while searching for food. From a wisdom perspective, criminals are more naive and less intelligent than birds. Their violence catches up with them. Eventually they fall into the same trap they set for others:

> they set a trap for their own lives.
> This is the fate of everyone greedy of loot:
> unlawful gain takes away the life of him who
> acquires it. (1:18, 19)

In short, crime doesn't pay.

The lesson has been learned. The motive for carrying it out is there. The folly of going with the bad crowd is clearly in view. The pupil has been well instructed. Now he can safely go on his way, armed with this invaluable knowledge.

Chapter 5

How Many Lesson Plans Are There? Overview and Broader Picture

> *The* instruction *has a unique structure of its own. The ten lesson plans, reminiscent of the Ten Commandments, are a gentle reminder that human wisdom falters when it does not stay close to God, the source.*

The wisdom teacher who did the final editing of the book of Proverbs included ten lesson plans within the first nine chapters. The thread that runs through them all is the motto "The fear of the LORD" as the beginning of knowledge or wisdom (1:7 and 9:10). Thus, all the nine chapters, and the ten instructions contained in them, are framed by this one single idea: if wisdom is not guided and directed ultimately by our relationship to God, it could miscarry.

Even the number ten, in the ten lesson plans, is significant. The Jewish reader would resonate to the number ten as a symbol of the Ten Commandments. It would remind him or her of the fact that obedience to God's commandments, as contained in the Torah, constitutes the highest wisdom. This indicates that

Proverbs 4:18 *"But the path of the just is like shining light,/that grows in brilliance till perfect day."*

the search for wisdom must be an integral part of faith in Yahweh and fidelity to his commands. For the Hebrew consciousness, the distinction between secular and religious wisdom practically does not exist. Whatever the origin of the separate collections, the wisdom sayings they contain find their ultimate meaning and fulfillment in the wisdom that comes from God.

The Ten Lesson Plans: An Overview

These are the ten lesson plans:

1. *A Warning Against the Wicked* (1:8–19);

2. *The Benefits of Wisdom* (2:1–22)

This chapter is written like a prospectus of a course on wisdom. It is a theme statement for many of the subjects that will be covered in separate discourses later.

3. *The Blessing of Fidelity to God* (3:1–12)

This instruction resumes the theme of fear of the Lord. Verse 1 mentions the Torah and the divine commands that should guide our search for wisdom.

4. *The Security That Wisdom Offers: Its Value in Society* (3:13–35);

5. *Wisdom as an Inheritance* (4:1–9)

The imperative given is: Obtain wisdom at all cost. It requires listening, obeying, and the trusting spirit of a child who heeds the words and commands of a parent.

6. *The Two Paths: The Way of the Just and of the Wicked* (4:10–19)

Both are easy to take. Only a strong and determined choice will make the difference. The only way to avoid the pitfall of the wicked path is: "Shun it. Cross it not."

7. *On Self-Discipline* (4:20–27);

8. *The Misery to Which Adultery Leads* (5:1–14);

9. *The Self-Destructive Folly of Adultery* (6:20–35);

10. *The Temptress: More on the Adulteress* (7:1–27)

Conclusion: The house of the adulteress, like the house of Dame Folly, is the way to Sheol. Do not enter it. It has the ring of evil foreboding, like the inscription over the gates of hell in Dante's *Inferno:* "All hope abandon ye who enter here!"

The Broader Picture
The First Instruction (1:8–19)

Theme: A warning against the wicked. Verses 10–12 describe a theft in the making. A preview of what the wisdom pupil is likely to face in the real world is in sharp contrast to the life of virtue that his schooling has inculcated in him. Virtue is held up as an ornament that one can lose if one is not careful and hangs out with the wrong crowd.

Context or Occasion: Perhaps the instruction is part of a graduating ceremony before the pupils go out into the world. The word for *diadem* (1:9) comes from the root meaning "to wind" or "to twist"; hence, a turban of some sort worn as a mark of authority or honor (cf. Ps 8:6; 2 Sam 1:10; Job 19:9). *Torque* (1:9) refers to a masculine adornment, made probably of wrought silver or beads. The pupils are being reminded of these marks of honor they will receive in society if they remain faithful to the teachings imparted to them. The moral principles they have learned from their parents and teachers will be their safeguard.

Lesson to Be Learned: Crime doesn't pay. The beginner needs to be reminded how easily he or she can be seduced into going with the wrong crowd. He also needs to be convinced how easily evil seducers fall into the same trap they lay for others.

The Clinching Statement: Birds are so naive that they easily walk into a trap while searching for food. The moral: criminals are even less intelligent than birds.

The Second Instruction (2:1–22)

Theme: The benefits of wisdom This chapter is a kind of prospectus for a course on wisdom.

Structure: The twenty-two lines of the poem are alphabetically arranged.[1] In the original they form one sentence, with an if-then structure. The content has a chiastic arrangement; that is, they form an A-B-B-A pattern. For example:

A Wisdom's Blessings	B Warning Against Evil Men
(vv. 1–11)	(vv. 12–15)
B Warning Against an Adulteress	A Promise of Blessings
(vv. 16–19)	(vv. 20–22)

Lesson: (1) Wisdom is more a gift from God than it is a human attainment. This is not to say that we can gain wisdom withou any effort on our part. It means that without God's help it would be difficult to come by the kind of knowledge, understanding, and insight that can guide right conduct. This is different from being "wise in their own eyes" (3:7). (2) Marital infidelity leads to idolatry and to death (physical or spiritual).

Purpose: Evidently the purpose of this chapter is to outline a program of what is to follow. Its several parts are later resumed in the subjects of separate discourses. For instance, Proverbs 1:12–15 sketches the way of the wicked. Their thinking and speech is crooked, quite the opposite of the upright and honest in 1:9. Evil has become so much their way that they can no longer be straight even if they want to. The whole chapter is a summary statement of topics that will be dealt with in greater detail in Proverbs 3–7, namely, evil men and the adulteress.

Contents of Chapter 2

"If" Part (vv. 1–4): Prerequisites for the successful pursuit of wisdom: eagerness in seeking it above all else and at all costs.

"Then" Part (vv. 5–22): Consists of authoritative admonitions in five parts:

(1) *vv. 5–8*—on the knowledge of God that comes with growth in wisdom and without which wisdom can't be had;

(2) *vv. 9–11*—on growth in moral understanding;

(3) *vv. 12–15*—on the resulting deliverance from the ways of wicked men;

(4) *vv. 16–19*—on escaping the seductions of "the adulteress" and "the strange woman";

(5) *vv. 20–22*—on the meaning and the rewards of an upright life.

The Third Instruction (3:1–12)

Theme: The blessing of fidelity to God. Chapter 3 picks up on the motto of the book (1:7) and the theme of the fear of the Lord covered in 2:5–8. This third discourse combines the outlook of (a) *Deuteronomy* that blessings come in return for fidelity with a spirituality centered on worship (vv. 2–3); and (b) *the Prophets*, especially Malachi (vv. 3:9 and 10).

Key: Echoes of traditional wisdom are present (long life), but emphasis is given more to a worshipful and prayerful attitude than to intellectual achievement: "In all your ways be mindful of him" (v. 6).

Structure: Consists of six quatrains beginning with an exhortation and promise of a special reward for obedience:

(1) *vv. 1–2*—Obedience and fidelity to teaching are rewarded with long life and well-being.

(2) *vv. 3–4*—Kindness and fidelity improve the quality of our relationship to parents and of a covenant relationship to Yahweh. It also makes us recipients of favor before God and men (Gen 47:29; Josh 2:1; Exod 36:9).

(3) *vv. 5–6*—Trust in the Lord and the Lord will keep your paths straight.

(4) *vv. 7–8*—Revere the Lord and you will have health of body.

(5) *vv. 9–10*—Honor the Lord with your wealth and you will prosper.

(6) *vv. 11–12*—Accept reproof and suffering as a discipline from the Lord; then you will gain the Lord's favor. This is a corrective to the idea that prosperity will always accompany piety.

The Fourth Instruction (3:13–15)

Theme: Wisdom's value in society to the security that wisdom offers:

(1) Increase in the quality of life, for wisdom confers strength and beauty, making the wisdom lover more attractive, like an ornament on a woman's neck (v. 22);

(2) Protection in all our undertakings (v. 23);

(3) Security of a restful repose (v. 26);

(4) Protection from fear against the sudden attacks of the wicked (v. 25);

(5) Assurance that the Lord is always by our side (v. 26).

Obligations of Dutifulness Include

(1) Giving speedy assistance to our neighbor;

(2) Doing him no harm;

(3) Avoiding unnecessary quarrels;

(4) Not envying or imitating a lawless man (ruffian).

Consequences That Follow: The just will enjoy God's favor; the wicked his disfavor.

The Fifth Instruction (4:1–9)— A Discourse Within a Discourse

Theme: Wisdom as an inheritance. The wisdom inherited from parents will pass on its blessings to the children (cf. Wordsworth's "Wisdom doth live with children round her knees").[2]

The Inheritance:

(1) Like a deeply devoted *parent,* wisdom will stand guard and watch over the individual always (v. 6).

(2) Like a *friend,* she will honor and cherish those who are faithful to her (v. 8).

(3) Like a *wife,* who is herself a jewel, she will bring glory to every aspect of a person's life (v. 9).

(4) Perhaps there is even a hint that, like a *queen,* she will bestow royal gifts and favors on servants and courtiers.

An Indispensable Condition: First, one must "get wisdom" (v. 7). This means that one must obtain it at all costs. It requires the listening, obeying, and trusting spirit of a child who heeds the words, commands, and counsels of the parent or teacher.

The Sixth Instruction (4:10–19)

Theme: The two paths.

Structure: The instruction is arranged in a chiastic form; it follows the A-B-B-A pattern, which we came across in 2:1–22:

A. *Way* of wisdom (vv. 11–13); B. *Way* of the wicked (vv. 16–17);

B. *Path* of the wicked (vv. 14–15); A. *Path* of the just (vv. 18).

Contrast:

(1) One leads to light and life; the other to darkness and death.

(2) One is straight; the other crooked and devious.

Comment: The artistic arrangement, the synonyms used for road, the action of stepping or running heighten the drama of having to choose one or the other path with utterly different and major consequences.

Key: "Shun it, cross it not." The strong command comes from the experience of generations: once a person gets into the grips of the temptation to evil, it becomes increasingly more difficult to extricate oneself from it.

Inspirational Thought: "But the path of the just is like shining light, / that grows in brilliance till perfect day" (4:18).

The Seventh Instruction: (4:20–27)

Theme: The discipline of listening with the heart (a self-discipline). The best way to secure the wisdom learned is to "guard your heart" (4:23). Above all, "deceitful speech put away from you" (4:24). Speech betrays the real directions of a person's heart (4:24–27).

Key Verse: "With closest custody, guard your heart, / for in it are the sources of life" (4:23). Its companion verse is: "Put away from you dishonest talk, / deceitful speech put far from you" (4: 24).

The Core of the Discipline (4:25): The virtuous man fixes his eyes upon the goal. He lets nothing turn them aside: "Turn neither to right nor to left, / keep your foot far from evil" (4:27). Virtue stands in the middle. One can deviate to the right by excess of zeal, or to the left by apathy and indifference.

Comment: Proverbs 4:20–27 reinforces the message of the two paths. It warns against straddling the fence between the two paths. The temptation of toying with a few sinful pleasures while trying to maintain an ethically upright lifestyle is dangerous. The wisdom teachers warned against the attitude of trying to have it both ways. A decision must be made. Our every effort must be directed toward attaining integrity and uprightness in our lives.

The Eighth Instruction (5:1–14)

Theme: The misery to which adultery leads. If unguarded speech can be the greatest internal enemy, the lures of an adulteress are the greatest external enemy. Proverbs contains four warnings against the adulteress (2:16–19; 5:1–14; 6:25–35; and 7:5–27). The woman alluded to is "a foreign woman" (cf. note on AB 2:16). This is a veiled reference to the fertility cults in honor of the goddess of sexuality, such as Ishtar (Babylonian) and Astarte (Canaanite). Many have thought that frequent references to "a foreign woman" in Proverbs 1–9 is a metaphor for apostasy, resulting from dangerous exposure to fertility cults.

Content: Four separate statements contrast the evil woman with the faithful wife:

(1) *vv. 1–6*—describe her words. Their smoothness is matched by their evil intent to trick the youth into acts of indiscretion that lead eventually to death itself. Discretion (v. 2) is the only safeguard.

(2) *vv. 7–14*—describe the sad consequences: (a) loss of the youth's good name; (b) his financial standing threatened by penalty payments to the husband or to the wife for her

favors; (c) his bodily health ruined by disease and by punishment (v. 11). At last remorse sets in.

(3) *vv. 15–19*—In contrast these verses use the metaphor of fresh water from one's well to describe a faithful wife.

(4) *vv. 20–23*—draw the moral conclusion: why go after forbidden pleasure that brings one to grief (death or loss), when one can be refreshed with faithful love? Verse 21 hints that God sees and judges our evil actions.

Note: The figure of a woman as spring satisfying sexual thirst is developed in Song of Songs (4:12, 15). That a cistern was privately owned (2 Kgs 18:31; Jer 38:6) gives point to the metaphor.

The Ninth Instruction (6:20–35)

Theme: The self-destructive folly of adultery. Adultery is the shortest-enjoyed and the longest-paid-for evil act in wisdom literature.

Punch Line (v. 32): "But he who commits adultery is a fool."

Explanatory Note: The light that guides is the divine revelation and the profession of faith in Yahweh that goes with it (cf. Deut 6:7–8; 11:19; Ps 119:105). But in Proverbs it is the moral lessons of Israel's wisdom traditions as contained in the discipline of moral instruction (6:23).

Content: Adultery with a married woman is condemned on many grounds:

(1) Sexual indulgence springs from unbridled lust. Hence it is morally wrong.

(2) As a violation of another's marriage rights it constitutes an act of injustice. That makes it even more reprehensible.

(3) It invariably ends in hurting all parties, including the betrayed husband. Verses 27–29 compare marital infidelity to playing with fire that carries with it the risk of being burned or scorched.

Verses 30–35 make the disparaging comparision between stealing and adultery. People will sometimes sympathize with a thief because of the desparate need that drives him to steal. However they will not make any allowance for adultery because it assaults the very foundations of marriage and undermines the stability of society. In addition to the punishment and monetary loss, which, like a thief, he is justly made to suffer, the adulterer is denied any standing or respect in the community.

The Tenth Instruction (7:1–27)

Theme: The temptress. More on the adulteress.
Content:

(1) Wisdom as a guide to life (vv. 1–5).

(2) A vivid description of the seduction of a youth by a married woman (vv. 6–20). She acts like a cultic prostitute who goes out in search of clients. The young man in turn moves closer in her direction. There he finds her waiting as she looks out of her trellised window.

(3) Verses 22–23 compare the youth who is beguiled into committing indiscretions with a woman to dumb animals like the ox, the stag, and the bird. They are silly enough

to wander into places where they succumb to their death. The seductive words of the woman are like the gaping jaws of death (Sheol) which are waiting to swallow the guilty alive. The imagery is borrowed from Canaan. With this instruction in the background, how compelling the proverb becomes: "The nether world and the barren womb; / the earth, that is never satisfied with water, / and fire, that never says, "Enough!" (30:16). How easily can passion ignite the fire of lust!

Conclusion: The house of the adulteress is the way to Sheol, as is the house of Dame Folly (2:18; 5:5; 7:27; 22:14).

Note on 7:1–5: Like Luke 6:20–24, Proverbs 7:1–5 cites Deuteronomy 6:4–9 as divine law and urges the readers to make wisdom teaching as much a part of their lives as a sister or close friend would be.

Chapter 6

The Fear of the LORD—
The Thread That Guides Them All

"Fear," reverence for God, putting God first in our lives, makes us think, say, and act in ways that others come to recognize as exemplifying wise conduct. The fear of the Lord provides the theme for framing the book of Proverbs.

The question may be asked: Why is the fear of the Lord said to be the beginning of wisdom? Why did the sacred writer, who did the final editing of the book, use this motto to serve as an inclusion, both to the first nine chapters (1:7 and 9:10) and to the entire work (1:7 and 30:31)? It was his way of saying that, whatever nuggets of wisdom the young trainees were to receive, they have their ultimate source in God.

But why "fear"? Surely God wants us to love him, not fear him. So fear cannot mean a frightened obedience to God in order to avoid punishment. Rather it has more to do with a sense of reverence we ought always to have in presence of the awesome majesty of God and of God's tremendous power. There is, of course, a healthy fear of the consequences of sin, but there is also a love and

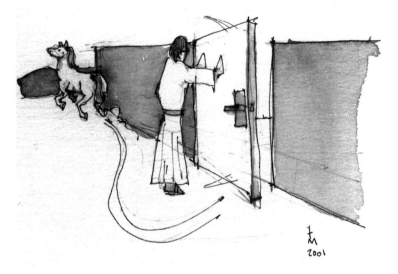

"It is too late to lock the stable door when the horse is already stolen." This proverb from an earlier equestrian culture prompted the adaptation in Proverbs 14:4.

trust in the divine power that cares for and directs all things in our lives. By putting God first in our lives, as a fundamental attitude of our spirituality, we are in fact putting ourselves under God's guidance and direction in all we think and do. And that is wisdom.

In 2 Kings 17:27, we are told that priests had to be sent to Samaria to teach the new settlers how to "fear the LORD," that is, to be good Jews. This meant living out their covenant relation to Yahweh through a faithful observance of his law (Torah). In the Deuteronomic as well as in the later wisdom tradition, the law was a path to wisdom (Deut 10:12; Ps 4:10–12). Proverbs emphasizes the point that one who tries to live an upright life before God

50

soon learns to think, act, and speak in ways that others can see exemplify living wisely. Ultimately, then, wisdom's source can be traced back to obedience to God, which is fear of the Lord. Since Yahweh has the ultimate say in our lives, it would be sheer folly to disregard his word and its teachings.

But there is another reason the wisdom writer chose "fear of the LORD" as the motto that should guide all discourse and teaching on wisdom. The phrase represents Israel's way of integrating secular advice into its religious tradition. So many of the wisdom sayings in Proverbs are of such a practical nature that we fail to see why they have found a place in the Bible at all. After all, much of the advice is sheer common sense: don't be lazy; work hard; stay out of trouble; don't run with the bad crowd; be careful with your money; stay out of debt; don't break your promises; guard your speech. So much of what common sense tells us to be true the wisdom writer has managed to enshrine in simple and beautifully crafted wisdom sayings. In the process of collecting its own proverbs, Israel found that they had much in common with the wisdom traditions of the ancient Sumerians, Assyrians, Babylonians, and Egyptians and even some of their surrounding pagan communities, such as the Canaanites. In borrowing sayings from other cultures, the wisdom teachers of Israel reworded some of them to suit their own cultural experiences. For instance, among cultures that used horses, we might come across a saying like "It is too late to lock the stable door when the horse is stolen." To bring this saying closer to Israel's experience, it might be reworded: "What use is it to close the manger once the oxen have gone out?" (14:4 AB). And even though a person who never thought about God could come to such commonsense conclusions, it is not true that those conclusions have nothing to do with our relationship to God. For the Israelites, who were called to live in a covenant relationship with Yahweh, no choice could be outside the context of covenant love. Why? Because they knew that our plans for success have a chance of being more secure when we are in the right relationship to God. God controls our destiny more than we do. Proverbs 21:2 says: "All the ways of a man may be right in his own eyes, / but it is the LORD who proves hearts." Israel's way of recognizing that God comes first in any decisions we make about what is good or best for us is to say, "The fear of the LORD is the beginning of knowledge."[1]

There is yet another and more profound way of understanding why God, or the reverence for who God is, must always direct our search for wisdom. When we observe God's creation, we see that God has created an orderly universe. All wisdom literature, including pagan literature, recognizes that there is an order in creation. If one perceives creation, one perceives order. The truly wise person is one who observes creation, reflects on how all the many parts work together to bring about a harmonious universe, and discerns that even our own lives, and our behavior, must be regulated by order. Our very place in the universe requires this. To recognize our true limitations as creatures is to have fear of the Lord." Echoes of this teaching resound throughout Proverbs: "The beginning of wisdom is the fear of the LORD, / and knowledge of the Holy One is understanding" (9:10).

This recognition becomes the moral undergirding for all other choices: the way we treat money, time, drink, friends, the poor, other people. All of these reflect our understanding of the order of things as created by God. All wisdom literature rests on the premise that observation and reason are necessary for discovering wisdom. But wisdom literature does not teach that observation and reason are necessary and sufficient to possess wisdom. God, as the author of all created nature, must be taken into account in planning out all our decisions.

This is particularly true with regard to decisions that are unavoidably based on choice. Time and again the lessons of the great wisdom teachers remind us that actions have consequences. They affect us as well as others. It is therefore the height of prudence that, in all our undertakings, and especially in the relationships we cultivate, we should be guided by fear of the Lord. Only then will we be able to recognize God's presence in the outcome of events.

The limitation to our ability to determine our own fate by ourselves is clearly evident in Proverbs. For one thing, we all need counsel. We need a wisdom teacher. We need God. Even in the simple matter of choosing a wife. we need God's help: "Home and possessions are an inheritance from parents, / but a prudent wife is from the LORD" (19:14). The frequent warnings against adultery, and the equally frequent advice of staying faithful to one's wife, undergird the truth that "a prudent wife is from the LORD."

The same acknowledgement that God is in charge is seen in the teaching against revenge: "Say not, 'I will repay evil!' / Trust in the LORD and he will help you" (20:22).

Human beings may travel the way of the wise or choose the road that leads to folly. The decision, however, to go one way or the other is not the sole determiner of the eventual outcome: "Many are the plans in a man's heart, / but it is the decision of the LORD that endures" (19:21).

The process of integrating secular wisdom into Israel's understanding of God's role in the universe is embodied in the phrase "the fear of the LORD." Only when we are truly in awe of God, and of God's order, will we make wise choices in the ethical and secular areas of our lives. An illustration of this truth is seen in the young shepherd boy in the Judean hills who pondered God's beautiful creation. Many of the inspired songs he sang in awe before the majesty of God have been recorded. They are among the richest treasures of wisdom for countless generations to come. This shepherd boy was David. His heart was always fixed on God (cf. Ps 57:8). He merited to become truly a man after God's own heart (cf. Ps 139:23–24).

David exemplifies the truth of Proverbs 23:17–18: "Let not your heart emulate sinners, / but be zealous for the fear of the LORD always; / For you will surely have a future, / and your hope will not be cut off."

Chapter 7

Wisdom's First Fall from Grace: The Tempting Adulteress Why This Obsession with Adultery? Is There a Catch?

Sexual indulgence is the pivotal sin that paves the way for every other kind of evil. It is a fast track to destruction and death. The seekers after wisdom must be forewarned of the danger. Lady Wisdom, the feminine side of God, has its counterpart in Dame Folly, who symbolizes the adulteress and all that is evil.

In the programmatic contents of Proverbs 2, we were given a preview of wisdom's specific mandate. It was to save "you from the way of evil men" (2:12). But even more, and perhaps with greater intensity and insistence, to save "you from the wife of another, / from the adulteress with her smooth words" (2:16). The warning against the tempting adulteress is repeated with mounting urgency in 5:1–14; 6:20–35; 7:5–27. Why this obsession with adultery? And what does it have to do with wisdom?

Proverbs 5:15 *A faithful marriage is described as drinking water from your own cistern.*

The first and obvious reason for the obsession is that adultery is a turning away from one's wife. Wisdom first found its sanctuary in the shelter of the home. It was there that love and trust abounded and wisdom's counsels were first offered and received. Within these sacred precincts, it was discovered that wisdom's nurture is at its best when a man is faithful to his wife and when their relationship of mutual love and trust is passed on to their children as a model to imitate. The longer the integrity of the home prevails, the greater is the possibility of wisdom taking deep roots. Wisdom promises a wonderful life to the man who remains faithful to his wife. A faithful marriage is described as drinking "water from your own cistern" (5:15). It offers a life full of intoxicating joy. Ingeniously enough, in the description of the faithful wife, the wisdom teacher has given us a picture of wisdom itself: "Her love will invigorate you always, / through her love you will flourish continually, / When you lie down she will watch over you, / and when you wake, / she will share your concerns; / wherever you turn, she will guide you" (5:19–22).

At the opposite pole of wisdom lie the temptress's "smooth words," her lying tongue, her crooked and deceitful ways, and the spell she casts. They rob the man of his innocence, his honor, his wealth, and, in some cases, even his life itself. Wisdom's warnings about the dire consequences of adultery follow the teaching of Deuteronomy: "If within the city a man comes upon a maiden who is betrothed, and has relations with her, you shall bring them both out to the gate of the city and there stone them to death...the man because he violated his neighbor's wife" (Deut 22:23–24). Wisdom's rich blessings, gained over long years of training, are lost in an instant and never fully recovered. The riches the man worked so hard to accumulate are dissolved in payments to the injured parties. Gone also are the reputation and security he enjoyed and the joy and peace, the guidance and comfort from his first and only true love. And then the specter of death hangs over the indelible scar of infidelity—if not actual death as prescribed by the Deuteronomic law, then surely eternal death for lack of repentance and restitution to the injured parties.

A second reason for the frequent warnings against adultery is that adultery is a turning away from wisdom. As we have just seen, many of the qualities that describe a faithful wife are also the qualities that characterize wisdom itself. As we continue to read Proverbs, we see wisdom personified as a woman. From a man's point of view, a woman is seen as being most desirable. Wisdom too is described as more precious than gold or silver, more valuable than corals or any precious gems. Her worth far surpasses that of wealth, riches, prosperity, or esteem; for wisdom is the very reason for their existence and the source from which they derive their value. So, in a way, all that is true of a faithful wife is also true of wisdom. She offers security just as wisdom does: those who seek her, we are told, will walk securely on their way. They will sit down and not be afraid. They will lie down and enjoy the repose of restful slumber (3:24). The bond between wife and husband is like the intimate bond that exists between wisdom and God. All the wisdom that has been accumulated through long training can be lost almost instantaneously by letting oneself be seduced by an evil woman. Adultery is therefore an act of sheer folly. Once the sanctity of marriage has been violated, it becomes the seed bed for every other kind of infidelity. No amount of warning can be deemed sufficient where the power of seduction is so great and the exposure to temptation so imminent.

A third reason adultery is wisdom's first fall from grace is that adultery is a turning away from God. In Canaanite religious practice, sexual relations with priestesses were not uncommon. The Mosaic law forbade Israelites, as God's covenanted people, from participating in cultic practices that honored other gods. To sleep with a cult prostitute would involve a double infidelity: to one's wife as well as to God.

In all probability, the woman who entices the young man to adultery in Proverbs 7 is a priestess or, at any rate, a cultic prostitute.[1] She says: "I owed peace offerings, / and today I have fulfilled my vows; / So I came out to meet you, / to look for you, and I have found you!" (7:14–15). Part of her cultic duty is to go out in search of clients and bring money into the temple by soliciting them. By painting a graphic picture of her intentions, as well as of the dire consequences that follow, the wisdom teacher, who is wisdom herself, hopes to deter her client from the road that leads to death. She (wisdom) warns: "Her house is made up of ways to the nether world, / leading down into the chambers of death" (7:27). In the mind of a pious Jew, adultery easily leads to idolatry, a whoring after other gods, and is punishable by death. On the other hand, marital fidelity is a practical way of demonstrating fear of the Lord, which is the beginning of wisdom.

Is There a Catch?

In all these frequent warnings against adultery, is there a catch? Could it be that, in the mind of the wisdom teacher, there is a hint of some hidden counsel that the prospective client must take to heart? It should be noted that, in all of these examples of sexual indulgence, the advice given is one-sided. The young man is warned against enticement from a tempting adulteress. His own responsibility is not mentioned. He is never instructed about his own sexual desires. Nor is he warned against enslavement to his own sexual passions. The training is strictly for males by males. Also the fidelity of the faithful wife is taken for granted. If anyone falters, it is more likely to be the husband, not the wife. What is the catch? Are the sages perhaps suggesting that, if a woman wants to keep the man she loves, she should do everything to keep him out of the reach of a conniving woman? If so, is this really sane advice? Would not such a ruse deflect from the wisdom already built into the picture of a faithful wife? If demonstrations of wisdom require the use of such clever trickery, does that not imply that the ideal wife was not so ideal after all? And why put all the burden of fidelity on the woman? Listen to what Proverbs 23:27–28 has to say: "For the harlot is a deep ditch, / and the adulteress a narrow pit; / Yes, she lies in wait like a robber, / and increases the faithless among men." In any event, opting for adultery is a choice that leads to death. The repeated warnings in Proverbs 1—9 against the adulteress as leading the way to death (see 2:18; 5:5; 7:27; 9:18) are summarized in the graphic imagery of 22:14: "The mouth of the adulteress is a deep pit; / he with whom the LORD is angry will fall into it." Wisdom warns that even God cannot be indifferent when the divine order he has established is undone by one act of adultery. By giving us a preview of the dire consequences of adultery, often with graphic comparisons, the wisdom teacher hopes to deter the seeker after wisdom from one of the worst pitfalls.

Chapter 8

Let's Take the "High Road" to Wisdom But Beware Who's Setting the Trap

---

The call to "higher wisdom," the wisdom that descends from above, is a comforting reminder that, in our bid for wisdom, we cannot make it alone. Wisdom's call is first discerned in the voice of reason through parents and teachers. When that fails, the prophetic voice of wisdom is heard within the depths of the human spirit. This higher wisdom is not a human attainment, but it does require human discernment in order to be appropriated as a gift.

---

1. The "High Road" to Wisdom

There is a wisdom that is accessible to each and every human being. It is the fruit of human experience. It can be obtained through careful observation and sound reasoning. Such wisdom contains insights that are true for the most part. In time we begin to discover that what is true for us is also true for many. We might even come to expect that it may possibly be true for all. As these

Proverbs 8:33–35 *"Happy the man who obeys me, / and happy those who keep my ways. / Happy the man watching daily at my gates, / waiting at my doorposts; For he who finds me finds life, / and wins favor from the Lord."*

truths gain universal appeal, they become the common heritage of all, and they become enshrined in folk sayings and proverbs.

But there is another kind of wisdom that requires human discernment but is not of human origin. It descends from above. It is a gift of God. For this reason it is better described as "higher wisdom," as distinct from the more common or "traditional wisdom." In Proverbs 2:6 we read: "For the LORD gives wisdom, / from his mouth come knowledge and understanding; / He has counsel in store for the upright, / he is the shield of those who walk honestly." The most likely to come by such wisdom are those who lead an honest and upright life. The fruit of such wisdom is *discretion* in order to help us discern right from wrong, good from evil; and *understanding* to guard us against crooked ways and deceptive speech, as well as against seductions to sexual immorality (2:11–15, 16–17).

2. Wisdom's Divine Origin

In Prov 3:19–20 and 8:22–31, wisdom claims to have existed from the beginning. Before anything else was created, wisdom already was. The grand design of the universe, as well as the execution of that design, was the work of wisdom. As the first of God's creation (8:22), she accompanied and assisted God in creating everything else that came after her. "Then was I beside him as his craftsman, / and I was his delight day by day" (8:30). Wisdom's role as "craftsman" suggests that she played a very active part in the process of creation. Already the natural wonders of the heavenly universe had aroused Israel to acknowledge God's omnipotent power at work in human affairs. Wisdom's claim to be "the first born of his ways" and "the forerunner of his prodigies" (8:22) implies a prior claim to recognition over the heavenly bodies. If the Israelites could see in the stars and planets signs of God's goodness, does not wisdom demand as much acknowledgement for her value?

Wisdom's divine origin can therefore be seen in the ordering of creation. The fashioning of the universe, the harmonious workings of its parts, is an example of the divine plan at work (3:19–20). Wisdom's all-pervasive presence in the world is like the divine presence itself. From the world's magnificent design one can discern the "Designer Infinite."[1] From the wonderful order in creation and the intricate harmony of its parts one can see God's wisdom ordering all things well. Wisdom's voice is heard in the harmony of the stars, the smooth workings of nature, the regularity of seasons, the succession of crops, of rain and harvest, of sunshine and darkness, of night and day.

The nobility of her speech also betrays the aristocracy of her divine origin: "Give heed! for noble things I speak; / honesty opens my lips" (8:6).[2] The straightforward simplicity and honesty with which she utters her words have an unmistakable quality about them. They are recognized as marks of true wisdom. That is why they demand a hearing.

"I, Wisdom, dwell with experience, / and judicious knowledge I attain" (8:12)—that is her promise. And she has the ability to make good this promise. All the knowledge she poured forth in bringing about an orderly universe she can now infuse into our experience, guiding us to bring right order into our existence and into all our relationships.

If we carefully observe all that God created, we can learn something about the God who did the creating. So too, when we listen to the simple, honest, and upright words of wisdom, we can experience the order that begins to take shape in our lives and in our relationships (8:27–31). This clearly is the work of consummate divine art much more than it is the fruit of human accomplishment. One can see one's life neatly fall into place: everything in the right measure, at the right time, and in the right circumstance. God loves order. He used order when he made everything else, when he put the parts of creation in right relationship with one another. Can God's gift of wisdom wish anything less than to put order into our lives and to bring harmony into our relationships?

The same wisdom that established order in the universe is also at work bringing order among nations: "By me kings reign, / and lawgivers establish justice; / By me princes govern, / and nobles; all the rulers of earth" (8:15–16). Wisdom calls on all to heed her words so that this right order in relationships will be established. She carries her message on the public streets and at the city gates (8:2–3). She makes her message accessible to all, not just to the privileged few. All her words are righteous (8:8), in sharp contrast to the crooked ways and deceptive cunning of evil persons. To listen to wisdom is to experience right order taking shape in our personal life. To those who heed her voice she promises a personal relationship of love: "Those who love me I also love, / and those who seek me find me....On the way of duty I walk, / along the paths of justice" (8:17, 20).

These words of wisdom remind us of the call to covenant love that the prophets constantly made to the people. So long as God's people were faithful to covenant love, they were able to perform just and righteous deeds. But when they were unfaithful, they acted out the whore (see Isa 1:21).

Wisdom continues to offer her counsels, so that all may "gain resource," "judicious knowledge," and "the fear of the LORD" (8:5, 12, 13). If all would only heed her word, they would find the happiness their creator intended them to have and would win favor with God. "Happy the man who obeys me, / and happy those who keep my ways. / Happy the man watching daily at my gates, / waiting at my doorposts; / For he who finds me finds life, / and wins favor from the LORD" (8:33–35).

Wisdom is a divine attribute that God wishes to share with us. God intended right order in creation, among nations, and in all human relationships. To discern this order, and to choose to live within it, is to find wisdom.

The royal road to wisdom, and the knowledge of its kingly art, is made available to all, but the voices of folly are also busy at work laying traps along the way. Wisdom's soundless call to follow her is heard in the recesses of the human heart. There, in the innermost part of our being, where spirit communes with Spirit and "deep calleth unto deep,"[3] is her voice heard. But the voices of folly impact us where we are most vulnerable, at the door of our senses. In the immediacy of everyday experience, impressions from the outside world are constantly feeding our craving for greed, illicit sex, money, wealth, prosperity, self-indulgence, and everything that can gratify us. They also lure us into unguarded speech as well as crooked and deceitful deeds to protect our interests. All knowledge passes through our senses. The discipline of "listening with the heart" is the antidote to protect us from falling into these traps.

Chapter 9

The Discipline of "Listening with the Heart"

Wisdom's richest blossoms grow out of the seedbed of contemplation. Wherever folly lays her traps, above the din and clatter of street noises, wisdom's gentle whisper can be heard: "Listen," "Obey," "Watch," "Wait," "Find," "Win." This is how she tenderly woos us into the discipline of listening with the heart.

Throughout Proverbs the plea of the parent to the child, of the teacher to the pupil, has been to "listen!" to the words of instruction being given, to the wisdom being taught. This frequent and often dramatic summons to attention underscores the urgency of getting wisdom, of getting it at all costs. This is because wisdom is priceless. It is indispensable for living. No one should do without it. No one can afford to.

Now in Proverbs 8 wisdom, personified as a woman, steps in to reinforce the authority of the parent and of the teacher. "Does not Wisdom call?" she asks (8:1). This rhetorical question demands a strong and emphatic response. In Jeremiah-like fashion she

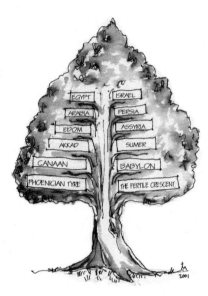

Proverbs 3:18 *"She (Wisdom) is a tree of life to those who grasp her..."*

assumes the role of a prophet, calling, pleading, urging each and all to become devoted seekers of wisdom. Even the foolish are invited to gain understanding.

Proverbs 8 represents an important editorial change. The wisdom teacher, who put the finishing touches to the collections of proverbs, inserted a wisdom poem in the middle of the two main literary genres that make up the book of Proverbs. It comes at the end of the lengthy, didactic discourses characterized by the instruction form (Proverbs 1—7). It precedes the shorter poetic parallel sayings known as the proverbs proper (Proverbs 10—31).

Moreover, the positioning of "Lady Wisdom,"—the woman par excellence—between the tempting adulteress in Proverbs 7 and her guiding spirit, "Dame Folly," in Proverbs 9 is also significant.

The Discipline of "Listening with the Heart"

Wisdom situates herself in strategic locations (8:2). Above the din and clatter of street noises, wherever folly lays her traps, wisdom's voice can be heard. Even when, under cover of the dark, the tempting adulteress stealthily goes on the prowl as if to lure her prey, wisdom's whisper reaches the heart. The greater the danger, the more urgent the need to offset that danger. Against the poison of sexual self-indulgence, whose effects can be far-reaching and even lethal, and of the frequent concessions to foolishness, the antidote of wisdom is made available to speed up the recovery.

Like the parent and the teacher, wisdom also invites us to "listen" to her plea; to ponder the inestimable blessings she brings; to contemplate the priceless treasures she offers: "Listen to my words." "Treasure them in your memory." "Wrap them up inside your heart." "Seal them on your lips." In words similar to these she makes her appeals (cf. 4:1–4; 5:1, 7; 6:2; 7:1–3; 22:17–18; 23:18). Listening and teaching go together, as do wisdom and contemplation. Listening is a heightened form of attention, of active receptivity, to what is being said. Listening opens up a wide range of activities for appropriating wisdom. These activities all come under the category of contemplation. We need to explore the connection between wisdom and contemplation.

1. Wisdom and Contemplation: *The Hidden Connection*

Wisdom has long been a favorite theme of contemplatives and mystics. This is perhaps because contemplation is the underground spring that nurtures wisdom. Contemplation occurs when the soul is most receptive. God takes the initiative and endows the soul with illuminations and inspirations. It is part of the Holy Spirit's gift of wisdom.

In Proverbs wisdom, personified as a woman, is "the first-born" of God's creation and the "forerunner of his prodigies" (8:22). She cries out aloud in the streets, in the open squares, down the crowded ways, and at the city gates (1:20–21). She invites all to come and partake of her sumptuous banquet (9:1–12). Contemplation is the activity of listening with the heart by which we gain access to wisdom's treasures.

Wisdom is priceless. Her worth far exceeds that of silver or gold. She far surpasses wealth and all other choice possessions. Wisdom enhances the quality of life, making it fruitful in every way, and bringing in its trail happiness, peace, prosperity, and all that makes life worthwhile. This is how Proverbs describes wisdom: "Long life is in her right hand, / and in her left are riches and honor; / Her ways are pleasant ways, / and all her paths are peace; / She is a tree of life to those who grasp her" (3:16–18).

Even though wisdom is necessary for living, not all are equally successful in finding it. This is partly because not all are sufficiently motivated in seeking it. Or they lack the discipline to strive after it. Or they do not have the discernment to recognize it when it is well within their reach. Or they lack the moral fiber to avoid the traps that lead to folly. The process of acquiring wisdom is long, and growth in wisdom is slow. But it takes only one act of indiscretion to be foolish. Wisdom demands a radical choice: life rather than death; light rather than darkness. Going one way is as easy as going the other, but the consequences are far-reaching. We cannot undertake the quest for wisdom alone. We need help.

The normal channels for communicating wisdom are parents and teachers. Instruction in wisdom begins in the home: "Observe, my son, your father's bidding, / and reject not your mother's teaching" (6:20). Even a bad parent can sometimes give good advice and administer wise counsels. But a virtuous parent, who exemplifies what he or she teaches, is an inspiring role model.

The surest way to wisdom is to be in touch with wisdom's ultimate source: God. However much intelligence, sound judgment, and resourcefulness may help, wisdom is ultimately born of the contemplative spirit. Proverbs 4:23 says: "With closest custody, guard your heart, / for in it are the sources of life." The heart is the metaphorical seat of contemplation. By fixing our gaze on God and pondering his holy word, the heart learns to absorb the mind and spirit of God and to appropriate his wisdom. Again and again we are being reminded, "The beginning of wisdom is the fear of the LORD, and knowledge of the Holy One is understanding" (9:10). Putting God first in our lives is the fundamental law of all spirituality. It is the moral undergirding for all other choices.

In the end, wisdom's counsel is: "Be not wise in your own eyes" (3:7), "Trust in the LORD with all your heart" (3:5). The emphasis is clearly toward a more meditative and prayerful attitude: "In all your ways be mindful of him" (3:6). Wisdom surrenders itself to one who has the trust, the simplicity, and the listening heart of a child. Wisdom is the fruit of contemplation.

2. A Wisdom Poem *(8:1–36):* *The Object and Activity of Contemplation*

Wisdom as Object

"Contemplation does not rest until it finds the object which dazzles it."[1] These words of Konrad Weiss aptly describe what the teacher-editor who composed the poem in Proverbs 8 may have been trying to convey. The object of the book of Proverbs is to teach wisdom. It demands knowledge, understanding, insight. The whole burst of fiery energy that consists in seeking, finding, and appropriating wisdom is called contemplation. This activity takes place at the deepest center of our being. It is an activity of the whole person. It does not rest until it finds its object.

"Get wisdom, get understanding!" (4:5) is the deep cry of the heart. Against the folly of following the path of the wicked, the voice of wisdom from within us cries out: "Shun it, cross it not" (4:15). The insufficiency of our own understanding often lies concealed by what is tawdry and false. But now and then this insufficiency bursts forth, reminding us that our ultimate recourse lies elsewhere, in the wisdom that never fails.

The wisdom poem introduces us to a profound paradox concerning the nature of wisdom. First wisdom speaks to us with the voice of reason and sheer common sense. She points out the value of wisdom for its own sake. She reminds us that wisdom is within our reach. It is a human attainment. We discover it as the voice of truth against all that is foolish, deceitful, and ultimately self-destructive.

The Discipline of "Listening with the Heart"

But as soon as we begin to take pride in our attainment, wisdom takes a higher ground. She reveals her royal connections (8:15–16). She offers to teach us the nobility of speech and conduct that befits kings. She educates us in the kinds of social graces that those in authority should have. In traditional wisdom such skills of public office were thought to be conferred on kings by God. The implication is that even though wisdom is of us, it is at the same time beyond us. It is something we clutch at as if it is our very own; yet it eludes us as soon as we become arrogant.

Verses 17–21 remind us that the only way to seek, find, and hold on to wisdom is to pursue it within an intimate relationship of love. To love wisdom is to become like her. It is in devotion to duty and in pursuing the path of justice that wisdom is most likely to be found (v. 20). She surrenders herself more easily to those who are drawn close to her.

Then, from verse 22 on, wisdom claims a divine origin. The poem suggests that every created good in some way reflects the wisdom of its Creator. Discovering this wisdom and putting it to practical use in our lives within a framework of moral order is the fruit of contemplation. Whenever our questing spirit receives a flash of insight, whenever a task is brought to successful completion, whenever a plan bears fruit, we recognize that a residue of divine wisdom is in us For the most part, much of wisdom comes to us after long seeking. It remains with us as long as we are humble enough to receive it and gratefully cherish it as a treasured gift. In the final analysis, the poem suggests that wisdom belongs more to the divine world than to the human world.

The Activity of Contemplation

The various nuances of contemplation are spelled out in Proverbs 8:32–36:

(1) The first is *listen.* "Listen to me," says wisdom in verse 32. The readying of the mind and the senses to observe, learn, absorb, understand what is being presented is listening. The whole focus of attention is directed to what is before us. In this case it is what the parent says, or the teacher tells us to do: "instruction and wisdom do not reject!" (v. 33).

(2) The second is *obey.* "Happy the man who obeys me, / and happy those who keep my ways" (v. 33). The root meaning of *obedience* (from the Latin *ob+audire*) is to hear someone out, to take into full consideration what is being said, or told, or asked of us. In obedience the activity of listening is carried one step further in that we do not make a decision or closure of judgment until the point, thrust, intent, and meaning of the discourse has been taken to heart and fully understood. Only then will the carrying out of the command or wishes become our own personal and responsible choice, at which point the act of obedience is complete. Then will the blessing be in place: "and happy those who keep my ways" (v. 33).

(3) The third is *watch.* "Happy the man watching daily at my gates" (v. 34). Wisdom sometimes comes to us as a presentiment before it becomes a reality. The anticipation of seeking what is within our reach keeps us on the lookout to see if we can discern the signs that point to it. Signs such as simple, honest, straightforward speech without any intent to confuse or confound; invi-

tation to virtue, to goodness, never to wickedness or evil; being open instead of being closed, devious, or deceitful.

Watchfulness also means being on the lookout for traps that are put in our way in order to lead us away from doing what we know is right. It means being vigilant to see that our success does not get in our way through pride or arrogance, that our wealth does not work against us through greed, strife, or the infliction of suffering or injustice on others. Watching means to let our experiences teach us to discern the folly of our ways. Watchfulness puts us on guard not to trust in ourselves, for fear that the wisdom gained may be lost as quickly as it was found. Watchfulness cautions us not to put our trust in the fast talker, the one with golden words and lying lips and deception in the heart. It warns us not to go the way of the wicked lest we end up falling into the pit that they have dug for us. Watchfulness alerts us not to make wealth our goal lest it disappear before our very eyes. Watchfulness helps us to discern that when we act wisely, we have the feeling that a debt of gratitude is owed, a debt that is impossible to repay; that wisdom, as it were, possesses us rather than we possess wisdom; and that we are the recipients of transcendent generosity. To be wise is to humbly acknowledge how truly blessed we are.

(4) The fourth is *wait*. "Happy the man.../ waiting at my doorposts" (v. 34). Waiting is a heightened anticipation that something good is about to happen; that what we have been looking for is nearer to us and well within our reach. Our experience tells us that wisdom does not usually come to us swiftly and easily. We go through periods of trial and error before wisdom

begins to dawn on us at last. If we didn't wait, if we stopped antic-
ipating, if we gave up the search, a golden opportunity could be
lost. Waiting is least of all listless passivity, hoping for something
to turn up. It is intense activity. It engages the whole energy of
our being toward a desired outcome, which at first is dimly seen
and then clearly perceived and understood. Watching was from
afar, from "outside the gates," toward the distant horizon. Waiting
is nearer "the doorstep." It is almost as if we had one foot inside
the door and we are about to enter wisdom's chamber, keeping up
the metaphor of wisdom building a house.

(5) The fifth is to *find*. The chase is over. Our search has
ended. We have found what we were looking for. Wisdom deliv-
ers itself to us as a prey to the hunter. Experience has taught us the
lesson we needed to learn. The teacher has gotten through to us.
He has succeeded in igniting the inspiration that can guide our
steps in the right direction and open the door to the future. The
parents' counsels have been found to be true. As a result, we have
become the wiser for it. By dint of effort we have steadily stayed
the course others have mapped out for us. At last we have found
"our way," which is also wisdom's way. In the process we have
earned a blessing: "He who finds me finds life" (v. 35). Life and all
that makes life worthwhile is what wisdom offers us. Our lives
have become richer, fuller, and more meaningful because of it.

(6) The sixth is *win*. From earthly happiness we are given a
foretaste of heavenly bliss. We have received much more than life
could possibly offer. We have won "favor from the LORD."

We began the journey early in life at our mother's bended
knee. There we learned the first lesson, that in all things the fear

of the Lord was to guide us. We listened, learned, obeyed, watched, waited, and found. We looked for the gift and found the giver. We were chasing the reflection and were able to trace it back to its luminous source. The crowning act of this journey is that we have won favor from the Lord. This blessing establishes us more securely under divine protection in all of life's circumstances over which we have no control. Our guidance doesn't cease because we have exhausted the limits of human ingenuity that were open to us. We are now on a higher plane. We are able to see life from a higher vantage point. From where we stand, we can clearly see that much of what we thought to be clever was in fact foolish. We can see the error of our ways and appreciate the moments when we surpassed ourselves by achievements not entirely of our own making. We are at the point where grace and nature meet. This is where our own insufficiency and the depth of wisdom come together and contemplation bears its richest fruit. Contemplation abides restfully in the object until the object becomes more clearly manifest to its gaze.

Wisdom needs to be caught, even more than it needs to be taught. Only in contemplation is this made possible.

Chapter 10

You Are All Invited to a Banquet Find Out: Who Is Lady Wisdom? And Who Is Dame Folly? Fill in Their Profiles, Please

---

Banquets are often given for soliciting clients. The character and caliber of a person are tested in the table talk. The way the banquet is prepared and what is being served are also a test of the hospitality of the giver. The wisdom seeker needs to know the difference so as to discern who is offering wisdom and who folly.

Wisdom's instructions have been given in the shelter of the home and in the protective environment of a school setting. Now Lady Wisdom herself must come down from her exalted place to give the instruction. First, she comes as a teacher, imparting instruction through the lips of the parent. Then she puts aside reason and persuasive argument and assumes the role of a prophet to reinforce, with the voice of her own authority, what the parents have taught. Then she unveils her identity and origin as "the first-

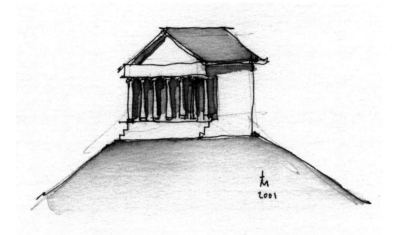

Proverbs 9:1 *"Wisdom's house is built on seven columns."*

born" of creation—a messenger of God speaking with divine authority (Prov 8:22).

There are other guises wisdom assumes in order to woo her way into our hearts. Like a devoted parent, she will watch over and protect us for life (4:6). Like a friend, she will honor and chreish those who are faithful to her (4:8). Like a faithful wife, who is herself a jewel, she will bring glory to every aspect of a person's life (4:9). Perhaps there is even a hint that wisdom, like a queen, bestows royal gifts and favors on servants and courtiers.[1] All this is but a prelude to the hospitality she has prepared by inviting us to a banquet (9:1–12).

Before we can partake of the sumptuous fare she has in store for us, let us briefly savor the glimpses of wisdom that the instructions have laid bare for us.

Wisdom's praises have been sung (3:13–35). Her blessings have been extolled (2:1–22). Her noble pedigree and ancient lineage have been traced (3:19–20 and 8:22–31).

Among her benefits are the honor she confers; the peace and security she offers, including restful repose in sleep (3:24); the protection she gives from fear, or harm, or loss of any kind; the health, well-being, and prosperity tempered by wholesome discipline she brings. All these are summed up in the metaphor of wisdom as "a tree of life" (3:18). "Long life is in her right hand, / in her left, riches and honor" (3:16).

Her speech is straightforward, her message true. Her paths lead to light and life. All this and more is ours just for the asking. We only need to heed wisdom's counsel: "Get Wisdom" (4:7). We must obtain it at all costs. That will require the listening, obedient, and trusting heart of a child.

The way of folly has also been mapped out in the instructions (4:14–19). Warnings have been given against the traps that Dame Folly has cunningly laid for us: unguarded speech, the seductions of sexual indulgence, especially with another's wife, the lure of ill-gotten gain. Against these pitfalls the simple and the unwary are asked to take precautions and to exercise the self-discipline of listening with the heart: "With closest custody, guard your heart, / for in it are the sources of life" (4:23). And yes, the companion to this discipline of the heart is the guarding of our speech (4:24), for speech betrays the real directions of a person's heart.

Wisdom descends to dispel our foolishness so that we in turn might ascend with her into the insights of divine knowledge. As

4:18 states: "But the path of the just is like shining light, / that grows in brilliance till perfect day"

There are, then, two distinct paths (4:10–19): the way of the just (wisdom) and the way of the wicked (folly). The one leads to life and light; the other leads to darkness and death. The one path is straight; the other is crooked and devious. Walking is as easy on the one path as it is on the other. Only our decision will make the major difference. It is not by accident that the simple, the unlearned find themselves on the one or the other path. They each travel along the road they have chosen, by heeding the invitations of Lady Wisdom or by following the frequent solicitations of Dame Folly.

So, at last, we come to the parable of the Two Banquets (9:1–18). One is given by Lady Wisdom.[2] The other is given by Dame Folly. What do these two have in common?

(1) *Both sit by the road and call people in.* As on many a previous occasion, Lady Wisdom has sent out her cry, sounded her call, and insistently sought out clients, pupils, candidates for wisdom (1:20; 8:1–4; 9:3). They have heard her cry in the streets, along the road, in open squares, in entryways, along crowded walks, at crossroads, and even at the city gates. She is willing to carry her treasures as far as it will take to catch a listening ear. But Dame Folly does not have to go that far. She cries out from her doorsteps. She invites the unwary passerby to partake of her seductive pleasures, which she readily displays in a show-and-tell fashion.

(2) *Both appeal to the simple.* These are, for the most part, people without much education or experience of the world. Yet they have enough curiosity to learn whatever might advance their

opportunities in life. They may or may not always be able to discern right from wrong. They may even venture to take a little risk for some gain. Lady Wisdom will make her appeal in a forthright and honest manner. She will call their attention to what is right and decent and honest and true (8:5–9). She will try to elevate their minds to what is more precious than gold or silver or the most prized corals or jewels. She will speak plain words to show that she is worthy of attention. Dame Folly will use devious and crooked ways to "sell her wares." She will use smooth and deceptive language, appealing to their baser instincts. She will offer the quick and ready pleasure that will satisfy their instincts for greed or self-indulgence (9:14–15, 17).

(3) *Both offer a rich reward.* Lady Wisdom will offer "instruction in preference to silver, / and knowledge rather than choice gold" (8:10–12). She will breathe into them her spirit and put her words in their mouth so that, with fear of the Lord in their heart, they will remove themselves from all hatred and evil (8:13). She will display her royal connections by teaching them the knowledge by which kings and nobles govern (8:15). She will lavish on them riches, honor, and prosperity, more priceless than gold (8:18). Dame Folly's reward will be the bread of unlawful gain and the drink of forbidden pleasures (9:17). But the house of folly is the grave that holds entombed all who enter. Her guests end up in Sheol (9:18).

Wisdom's superiority over folly needs no demonstration. It only needs to be discerned by an honest and upright heart. Her clientele are those who obey her and keep her ways (8:33). But Lady Wisdom's banquet requires a long period of learning and discipline, honest search and tireless effort, On the other hand, the lure of quick pleasure and easy gratification offered by Dame Folly captures many.

We are now ready to fill in the profiles of both these seekers of clients.

The Portraits of Lady Wisdom and Dame Folly

Portrait of Lady Wisdom

Wisdom's house, built on seven columns (9:1), is distinct from folly's house set high on a hill (9:14). The number seven stands for completion or perfection. It means that wisdom is never wanting. It finds its perfect fulfillment in those who truly revere and worship the name of the Lord. Wisdom inhabits those who seek her. She finds her abode in those who "fear the LORD" (9:10). The seven columns may also stand for strong support: no sooner do we firmly commit ourselves to obey God's commandments and put God first in our lives than wisdom becomes securely established in us. Thus wisdom's house is symbolized by Jerusalem's temple. Those whose hearts' yearning is to be close to the Lord, to dwell in the sanctuary of the Lord (Ps 84:5) as David did, will find wisdom to be their constant companion. Wisdom's palatial abode is a metaphor for a storage house of rich treasures, which she bestows on those who eagerly seek her.

Lady Wisdom's character is that of a rich and virtuous mistress of a palace. Those invited to eat at her banqueting table must match her honesty, uprightness, simplicity, and sheer goodness.

Their speech must harmonize with their deeds and be free of guile, duplicity, or even the intent to deceive. Like God, whom she resembles and whose emanation she is, she can never act out of character. She is always true to herself. Being one of a piece with oneself and at peace with oneself is the very definition of simplicity, which God is. Wisdom is divine in her origin. She descends from above. Yet her double yearning is to be God's "delight day by day" (8:30) and at the same time to find "delight in the sons of men" (8:31). In some marvelous and mysterious manner she bonds God with his creation, most of all with his human creation.

The sumptuous banquet, described in ritualistic symbols of sacrifice, comprises life and all that makes life rich and beautiful. "Forsake foolishness," she says, "that you may live" (9:6). In addition to life in its fullness, her viands consist of the "wine of wisdom" and the "bread of instruction." All that one can get out of life is captured in the fruitful insight that matures in us through knowledge and understanding of the Holy One, who is wisdom itself (9:10).

The fruit of wisdom is life in its fullness and all that makes life worthwhile. This includes such things as the honor and esteem that she enjoys before God and men, together with riches, wealth, prosperity, security, peace, and good relationships in our family and our social enterprises.

Portrait of Dame Folly

Keeping up her parody on wisdom, Dame Folly also maintains a house on a high hill.[3] The way she maintains and runs her house, however, is markedly different from that of Lady Wisdom.

Her operations are more reminiscent of temple cult prostitutes and their sexual rites, which have a pagan origin. The pleasures she offers remain hidden and clandestine. For that very reason they heighten their seductive quality. It is enough to give but the merest furtive glimpse of her hidden secrets, only to leave the hungry client begging for more. She adroitly positions herself at her doorstep and sets the trap for the unwary passerby.

Unlike Lady Wisdom, Dame Folly is "boisterous, ignorant (or inane) and shameless" (9:13 AB). The vulgarity of her speech and demeanor match her deeds. Being located "outside the temple," her behavior is no longer protected by moral codes. Thus she can afford to be openly profane (from *pro* = "in front of or outside" and *fano* = "temple"). She has no qualms about disengaging the seeker after wisdom from its source: the fear of the Lord. Once the client can forget, for even the briefest moment, that God exists or counts, he is free to do whatever he likes. Once he has taken the first timid steps in her direction, under cover of the dark (7:8–9), she goes out to meet him. She turns on her seductive charms and lures him into her chamber (7:10). Free from the restraints of any moral code, he wallows in utter licentiousness. Adultery easily leads to idolatry; the two words come from the same root.

Like Lady Wisdom, Dame Folly also offers a sumptuous banquet. She spreads her feast of "stolen water" and "bread gotten secretly" (9:17). These are metaphors for secretly engaging in sexual pleasure with another's wife (cf. 5:15, 20). The description of the banquet fits in with her character as a loose, wanton, or fickle woman (9:13). Here she represents vice in general; but in the mind of the sage, impurity stands first among the vices.

One learns only too late that such self-gratification leads only to death. In wisdom literature, as mentioned, adultery is the shortest-enjoyed and longest-paid-for evil act. To engage in such behavior must therefore be judged sheer folly.

The "simple" are invited to both banquets. However, being simple covers a wide range of meanings. It can mean being trusting, open, honest, ready to believe. It can also imply being stupid, naive, lacking discernment, and foolish. Simplicity can be a precious quality in that it helps make one an apt candidate for learning wisdom; and once securely under wisdom's guidance, the simple person could rapidly advance in knowledge. On the other hand, the simple can also be an easy target for the trickery and duplicity that lie hidden in the lewd advances of evil persons. Simplicity makes one an easy target or an apt candidate to take the one path or the other. Which path is taken will depend on the choice made. Wisdom teaches how important it is to secure the right choice early in life by forming strong convictions and good moral habits that wisdom's instructions provide. As 22:6 states: "Train a boy in the way he should go; / even when he is old, he will not swerve from it." Truly, the child is father to the man.

Chapter 11

Wisdom's Second Fall from Grace: The Lure of Money Is Wealth a Blessing or a Temptation? Who Will Write the Financial Column?

Wisdom promises prosperity. Wealth is not a matter of how much we have. It is more a question of how much we do with whatever little we have. Who we are before God and our fellow human beings is more important than being wealthy. In the pursuit of wisdom we discover certain qualities that attract or repel wealth. Wisdom teaching on wealth is pursued on three levels: common sense, moral uprightness, and spiritual insight.

By nature we come endowed with a capacity, and sometimes even a thirst, for wisdom. In living out our lives, we develop a skill for successful living. Some rare souls might even find themselves treading the path of higher wisdom, as a gift of divine bounty. As we become adept at living successfully and our endeavors pay off

Proverbs 9:17 *"Dame Folly's banquet consists of 'stolen water' and 'bread gotten secretly'—metaphors for secretly engaging in sexual pleasure with another's wife (Prov 5:15, 20)."*

in rich dividends of wealth, we might find ourselves succumbing to the lure of money.

So the question to ask is this: Is wealth a blessing or a temptation? Is it an asset or a liability? Is being wealthy a privilege or a pitfall? Before we can answer these questions, the case for wealth must first be carefully examined.

1. Three Layers of Wisdom Teaching Concerning Wealth

In the book of Proverbs, there are three distinct layers of wisdom teaching concerning wealth. They each mark a clear line of progression.

Wisdom's Second Fall from Grace: The Lure of Money

(1) The first takes a purely worldly, practical, commonsense look at wealth. Simply stated it is this: wealth is good; the lack of wealth is bad. Proverbs 13:8 says: "A man's riches serve as a ransom for his life, / but the poor man heeds no rebuke." This proverb makes the neutral observation that the possession of wealth frees us from many normal worries whereas poverty makes instruction almost impossible.[1] Another neutral proverb states: "The rich man's wealth is his strong city; / the ruination of the lowly is their poverty" (10:15). There is here a tacit admission that without wealth one cannot get on in life.

A similar thought occurs in 18:23: "The poor man implores, / but the rich man answers harshly." The helplessness of the poor, in not being able to get what they need, is contrasted ironically with the irritation that the more fortunate feel when asked to give away what they have worked hard to attain. The poor are outwitted at every turn: "Even by his neighbor the poor man is hated, / but the friends of the rich are many" (14:20). These sayings concede that the wealthy have it made. Proverbs 19:4 is rather forceful: "Wealth adds many friends / but the friend of the poor man deserts him." In the same vein 19:7 points out, "All the poor man's brothers hate him; / how much more do his friends shun him!" Society tends to look unfavorably on the poor because of the preconceived notion that poverty is the result of indolence. It takes the grim view that the lazy get what they deserve. The opposite notion looks at wealth as the reward of hard work (cf. 10:4; 11:26; 12:11; 14:23).

On a more positive note wealth is said to enhance the quality of life: "The just man's recompense leads to life" (10:16). Or again, "A man's riches serve as ransom for his life" (13:8).

In addition to providing the amenities of life, wealth also brings power, influence, and honor in society: "The rich rule over the poor, / and the borrower is the slave of the lender" (22:7). A certain measure of wisdom is always implicit in the successful management of wealth. Without wisdom wealth tends to disappear (17:2). No doubt, there is a measure of security that wealth offers (18:11). Wealth might well be a man's "strong city" provided he has the moral fiber to prevent his fancies from becoming disappearing bubbles in the air. We therefore need to carry our commonsense view of wealth to a higher level of discourse.

(2) At a higher level, moral considerations enter into the picture. Such considerations must guide the acquisition and the use of wealth. For instance, we are reminded that ill-gotten wealth is a fast track to death (10:2). We also read, "Wealth is useless on the day of wrath, / but virtue saves from death" (11:4). Proverbs 11:18 is even stronger: "The wicked man makes empty profits, / but he who sows virtue has a sure reward." The profits of the wicked are "empty," perhaps because they lack the inner character to make their riches last or to prevent them from being shamefully squandered away. Virtue evokes a certain level of trust required for a responsible handling of one's own or other people's money (13:21–22). Virtue attracts wealth; wickedness repels it (15:6).

Wickedness comes disguised under many forms. Greed is only one of them. Proverbs 15:27 admonishes, "He who is greedy of gain brings ruin on his own house, / but he who hates bribes will live." Rogues are trapped by their own cupidity. Greed enhances the precariousness of wealth (28:22).

Wisdom's Second Fall from Grace: The Lure of Money

Virtue seems to be an indispensable condition for acquiring and enhancing wealth. At all times virtue must precede and sustain the activity of becoming wealthy. In a manner of speaking, wealth is not only the reward for being virtuous; it is also the means for being generous and doing good to others. Without the well-ordered life that is the fruit of virtue, one lacks the power for holding on to one's wealth. Even "an intelligent servant will rule over a worthless son, / and will share the inheritance with the brothers" (17:2). Virtuous living prevents us from becoming enslaved to wealth and making it our master.

But can we be really sure that virtue will always prevail? What is there to prevent virtue from eroding under the seductions of wealth? Is there any other factor that can anchor virtue so securely and prevent wealth from becoming a trap? What can prevent all that nobility of effort that has built an empire of wealth from disintegrating under our very eyes? We have to contend not only against the insecurity of virtue, despite the tenacity of will to sustain it. We also have to reckon with the evanescent nature of wealth itself.

There are many proverbs that deal with the elusive nature of wealth. Proverbs 23:4 counsels us not to make wealth our goal. And Prov 23:5 tells us why: "While your glance flits to it, it is gone! / for assuredly it grows wings, / like the eagle that flies toward heaven." Fortune sometimes changes hands. The rich of today become the poor of tomorrow.

There are paradoxes of wealth that describe the varying fortunes of rich and poor alike. For instance, we are told, "One man is lavish yet grows richer; / another is too sparing, yet is the poorer" (11:24). Surprisingly enough, wealth increases when given away (28:27; 11:26; 11:25). It disappears when ill-gotten (10:2; 28:8). Even in the midst of wealth we are reminded of the insecurity of riches (11:28; 20:21). Generous giving is an antidote to greedy hoarding (21:26). Wealth has a tendency to return when given away, to disappear when held on to (22:9; 28:27). Proverbs 11:28 admonishes: "He who trusts in his riches will fall, / but like green leaves the just flourish." Despite every attempt on our part, we do not have full control over our wealth. Once we have grasped this fact, we are ready to move to a higher level of wisdom teaching concerning wealth.

(3) Having dealt with the practical and moral aspects of wisdom teaching, Proverbs goes on to consider the spiritual aspects. At this third and highest level of wisdom teaching, there is a dawning recognition that the Lord is the ultimate giver of wealth: "It is the LORD's blessing that brings wealth, / and no effort can substitute for it" (10:22). God's blessing is boldly and unequivocally affirmed over every human effort to climb the ladder of success. Wisdom recognizes God's role in the acquisition of wealth. Any sagacity, shrewdness, or resourcefulness we may possess must surrender to God's watchful and loving care over us and his provident designs concerning our worldly possessions. Our preoccupation should be more with the God who provides than with the wealth we own. Our administration of wealth must be guided more by the effort to please God than by a desire to please ourselves. Our priorities in the acquisition and use of wealth must be determined by our covenant relationship with Yahweh.

Wisdom's Second Fall from Grace: The Lure of Money

As we mature spiritually, we begin to experience a growing detachment from wealth. We come to realize that other things are more important. "Better a little with the fear of the LORD / than a great fortune with anxiety" (15:16). "Better a dish of herbs where love is / than a fatted ox and hatred with it" (15:17). "Better a little with virtue, / than a large income with injustice" (16:8). "How much better to acquire wisdom than gold! / To acquire understanding is more desirable than silver" (16:16). Such "better than" proverbs are timely warnings not to make wealth the entire focus of our lives. As the love of Yahweh grows deeper in our hearts, we are able to distance ourselves from the preoccupation with wealth and the worries that go with it. As God becomes the acknowledged giver of all we possess, our hearts begin to lean toward the giver rather than to be absorbed with the gifts.

Even our attitudes toward wealth and poverty become transformed. Wealth is no longer an unmixed blessing it once was, nor is poverty the dire misfortune we once thought it to be. "Rich and poor have a common bond: / the LORD is the maker of them all" (22:2). And again, "The poor and the oppressor have a common bond: / the LORD gives light to the eyes of both" (29:13). The rich and the poor are seen in a new light. The rich man's love for God makes him see the poor through the eyes of God. Since God loves the poor and the rich man loves God, he too in turn comes to love the poor.

His stewardship toward the poor flows out of, and is a manifestation of, his covenant love for Yahweh. Giving to the poor is like lending to the Lord (19:17). For the same reason, one who gives to the poor will be blessed (22:9). On the other hand, we are enjoined not to mock the poor or rejoice in their calamity (17:5). Nor are we to injure the poor or crush the needy. The reason given is that "the LORD will defend their cause" (22:23). There is even a blessing attached when we give to the poor. We are told that one "who gives to the poor suffers no want" (28:27). All the injunctions and blessings that wisdom lays out are already known to the heart of one who loves Yahweh. With our heart pointed toward Yahweh, we cannot go wrong, for ultimately "the tester of hearts is the LORD" (17:3).

In the light of this testing, the wealthy stand forewarned. The privilege of possessing wealth always carries the burden of sharing our treasures with the less fortunate. If one should succumb to the lure of wealth and resort to evil ways, then the roles of rich and poor could be dramatically reversed. So we are told: "Better a poor man who walks in his integrity / than he who is crooked in his ways and rich" (28:6). In a sense, the righteous poor are richer in the eyes of God than the unjust rich. The example of Dives and Lazarus is a case in point.[2] The wise man knows that ultimately wealth can be as much a burden as dire poverty. From the sage's mouth therefore comes this prayer of the enlightened heart. It is the prayer of a dying man: "Two things I ask of you, / deny them not to me before I die: / Put falsehood and lying far from me, / give me neither poverty nor riches;.../ Lest, being full, I deny you, / saying, 'Who is the LORD?' / Or, being in want, I steal, / and profane the name of my God" (30:7–8). In the end, death opens our eyes to the truth of things. The wisdom that should have guided us all along begins to dawn on us at last. If only we could look back at life through the eyes of death!

2. The Wisdom of Wealth Follows a Graded Path

Proverbs holds that wealth is good, virtuous living is better. But most important of all is the fear of the Lord.

As we mature in the art of successful living, we learn to see the hidden connection between wisdom and common sense, wisdom and virtue, and finally wisdom and faith. Without these three essential ingredients of wisdom, namely, common sense, virtue, and faith, wealth would be of little avail. So, in addition to the practical skills required for the attainment of wealth, wisdom also consists of the moral and spiritual qualities for making our wealth work for us, not against us.

The commonsense approach to wealth might well be part of an older collection of wisdom sayings. It consists of more neutral proverbs used for educating the young and the apprenticed public servant in the mastery of life. Such proverbs might well date back to a time long before King Solomon.

At a later stage, these neutral proverbs were modified, corrected, and refined by sayings that emphasize Yahweh's control over success and failure, thus establishing a close connection between wisdom and faith.

A possible middle stage between the older and later wisdom traditions would have been a developing awareness that moral attitudes are basic to divine order and that upright behavior is always rewarded.[3]

Thus, a long history of development has taken place. It is only in the final reading of the total collection that the message of proverbial wisdom for Israel can be clearly seen. The message contains keen observation of both practical and moral conduct and the consequences of human conduct with trust in God and reliance on the divine ordering of the world.

3. Who Will Write the Financial Column?

In the end, wealth, fortune, riches, substantial prosperity is not a question of how much we have. It is rather a question of how much we do with whatever little we have. Who we are in the eyes of our fellow human beings and of God is more important than what we have. It is almost a given that there are certain qualities in every person that attract or repel wealth. The kind of person people are likely to trust with their investments is one who is honest, trustworthy, dependable, just, and generous. He is one who is rewarded in proportion to the degree he is able to work for the benefit of others.

There is also the question of the wise and unwise use of wealth. Wealth requires careful stewardship on the part of the wise, in contrast to the lack of foresight and the shortsighted cravings of the foolish. So, we might say that lack of proper stewardship signals one of the major perils and pitfalls of wealth. What is not honestly earned can be easily squandered (10:2). Wealth that is tainted at the outset compounds its liability by the way it is used. What is wanting is the virtue that "saves from death" (10:2).

Proverbs holds out the promise that God will never forsake those who are faithful to him. The just may not have much. But they won't starve (10:3). Virtue binds wealth more securely to its owner for enhancing the quality of life. There is always love, peace, contentment, sweet repose in the house of the just, and there will always be sufficient food on the table. Unity and harmony among the members of the household will abound.

Another pitfall of wealth lies in the intention that it serves. The intention will mark off the wise from the foolish. So we might ask: What does the foolish person want? Strife seems to be one answer: "Hatred stirs up disputes, / but love covers all offenses" (10:12). Quick gain at someone else's expense is another. Violence is never far away from the ways chosen by such people, since they want what they want at any cost: "but the mouth of the wicked conceals violence" (10:11, 13).[4]

The goal of the wise is far different. It is life itself in all its richness: "The just man's recompense leads to life" (10:16). It is long-term: "Wise men store up knowledge." (10:14). When wealth is invested in proper education, it helps to enhance the quality of life itself. In addition to being long-term, it also requires careful learning: "A path to life is he who heeds admonition" (10:17). It also requires careful speech: "A fountain of life is the mouth of the just…" (10:11).

Ultimately, true wealth is the product of a good life. It is also the product of wisdom, which consists of right order in our relationships to God and to our fellow human beings. "The steps of a good man are ordered by the LORD, and he delighteth in his way. Though he fall, he shall not be utterly cast down: for the LORD upholdeth him with his hands" (Ps 37:23 KJV). The truly just-wise person has more staying power than all the market forces in the world. Such is the enduring promise that wisdom, both human and divine, offers.

Chapter 12

Wisdom's Third Fall from Grace: The Tripping Tongue Where Are All the Speech Writers?

Words are the currency of wisdom teaching. Its stated purpose is to make us "craftsmen of speech." Cultivating good speech requires that one be a good listener and a quick learner. One can learn to avoid the pitfalls of speech by paying heed to common sense, observing rules of moral integrity, and practicing obedience to God.

Proverbs is all about the wisdom of words. The proper use of speech is central to the wisdom tradition. This is clearly evident in both of its two main forms of communication: the instruction (Proverbs 1—9) and the proverb proper (Proverbs 10—31).

The Instruction

The earliest recorded use of instruction as a tool for teaching comes from ancient Egypt.

Proverb 61:1   *"Man may make plans in his heart,/but what the tongue utters is from the LORD."*

The *Instruction of Ptah-hotep* dates back to the third millennium B.C.E.[1] It tells us what a king might expect from his son. The son must set an example to the children of officials. In addition to acquiring the skill and poise proper to his position, he must learn "the rules of good speech."

Similarly, the *Instruction for King Merikare,* dating from 2100 B.C.E., emphasizes the need for becoming a "craftsman of speech." [2] The king's son must be taught the art of speaking the seasonal word: the right word, to the right person, at the right time, in the right place, and in the proper measure (cf. Prov 15:23; 25:11). Training in proper speech teaches him how to deal with persons with whom his official duties bring him into contact.

The Egyptian *Instruction of Amen-em-ope,* which dates back to between 1000 and 600 B.C.E., emphasizes the cultivation of good speech for making one's mark in life. It opens thus: "The beginning of the teaching of life, the instruction for success. All precepts for conversation with the great, the rules for courtiers, to know how to answer one who speaks, to return a written message to one who sends it." [3]

Hebrew instruction was also the normal means by which parents handed down the household mores and the ancestral tribal wisdom to their children. It recognized the value of proper speech: "Incline your ear, and hear my words, / and apply your heart to my doctrine; / For it will be well if you keep them in your bosom, / if they all are ready on your lips" (Prov 22:17–18). And again: "And my inmost being will exult, / when your lips speak what is right" (23:16).

But instruction as a finely developed art was an Egyptian import. It was introduced by King Solomon into the Hebrew wisdom schools in about the tenth century B.C.E. Speech training was once a kingly art, reserved for the officials of the royal court. Now, under the patronage of King Solomon, it was made available to all persons. "Winning speech" catches the ear of the king and even of Yahweh himself (22:11).

The Proverb

The Importance of Good Speech

By the time of King Solomon, proverbs had become part of the teaching curriculum in the wisdom schools. Even in these short, pithy, well-knit, mostly two-line sentences in parallel structure, great attention is given to proper speech by parent and teacher alike. Thus the parent might exhort the child: "And my inmost being will exult, / when your lips speak what is right" (23:16). Likewise the wisdom teacher often reminded his pupils, in the course of their training, "Like golden apples in silver settings / are words spoken at the proper time" (25:11). A long-standing tradition regards proper speech as a sign of intelligence, firmness of grasp, and possession of ancestral wisdom.

The utterance of wisdom is one of the main spiritual functions of speech (cf. 10:13, 31). Notwithstanding this lofty ideal, the tongue can be treacherous. It is the most unruly member we possess: "Death and life are in the power of the tongue; / those who make it a friend shall eat its fruit" (18:21). Wisdom is life-giving and folly is self-destructive (10:11, 14). The book of Proverbs underscores the value of good speech as well as the disciplines necessary for cultivating it.

The Value of Good Speech

Good speech is often compared to precious metals such as silver and gold (10:20; 20:15). It is precious (a) when it is expressed graciously and eloquently (25:11; 15:2; 16:21, 23; 22:11); (b) when it is beneficent (16:24; 15:26; 12:25); (c) when it is gentle (15:1, 15); (d) when it is "just" or open, even to giving a reprimand (10:10; 16:13; 25:12); (e) when it is honest and reliable (12:19, 22; 14:5, 25); (f) when it is timely (15:23); (g) when it nurtures (10:11; 13:4) or brings deliverance (11:9).[4]

The Disciplines for Cultivating Good Speech

First is the *discipline of listening*. Words are precious, but they are most savored when they flow out of a listening heart. In a stroke of antithetic parallelism, the "prating fool" is contrasted with the "wise man" who "heeds commands" (10:8). Proverbs is entirely about a son who heeds his parents' commands, a pupil who follows the wisdom teacher's counsel. The practice of this discipline begins very early in life (22:6). It continues through the formative years of training. The urgency of listening, so frequently expressed in Proverbs, is all the more important, given our proclivity to folly (14:7; 15:2). Listening is an acknowledgement of the need for, and the first step to, listening to God, the source of all wisdom (16:1, 9, 20; 20:27; 30:1–6). Listening leads to hearing; hearing to obedience (18:16; 22:17); and obedience to the rewards that wisdom brings. On the other hand, there is a price to pay for refusing to heed the word of wisdom (13:6).

Second, there is the *discipline of teaching*. In the hands of a skillful teacher, speech rises to an art form. "The wise man is esteemed for his discernment, / yet pleasing speech increases his persuasiveness" (16:21). Words are, after all, the currency of the wisdom school. Through mastery of the carefully crafted word, the teacher hands down the ancestral wisdom. Words spoken are words to be remembered and to be lived. Only then can instruction become fruitful (12:14; 13:2).

Third, speech also has its own discipline. So we come to the *discipline of speech:* the discipline of the carefully crafted word. Given the tight structure of the proverb, less is always better than more. Brevity must be matched by profundity. The terseness of the wisdom sayings reflects the view that wisdom is best expressed in a few rather than in many words. The goal is always to use a minimum of words with a maximum of meaning. This mentality is reflected in many of the sayings. Use words sparingly for whatever reason (10:19; 17:27). Think before you speak (15:28; 29:20). Or again, listen before you speak (18:13). Watch your tongue (13:3; 21:23). This all implies that one knows how to observe silence (12:16, 23). Words are more likely to be rich in meaning when they come from a reflective spirit and the depths of human experience.

The Pitfalls of Speech

Proverbs are a sad reminder that the tendency to foolishness is part of our human condition. "Knowing lips one meets with by surprise" (14:7). We are therefore admonished to take steps to avoid the company of foolish persons lest we become foolish. Equally are we reminded that walking with wise men makes us wise (13:20). By far the greater number of proverbs are about avoiding foolishness before it becomes an ingrained habit.

There is a fool that lurks inside all of us. Each of us is foolish some of the time. Some are foolish most of the time. Many are foolish all of the time. Folly is a matter of frequency and degree. The tendency to foolishness is all the greater as our discourse moves away from common sense, moral integrity, and obedience to God. These are the three tracks along which wisdom travels. They are also the pivotal points round which proper speech turns. The degree of foolishness must be measured against the three standards of common sense, morality and piety.

(1) *Common sense.* Speech should be in keeping with common sense. We should include in this category such qualities as civility, propriety, and decency. In every age society has regarded such qualities as appropriate to wise conduct. This is partly because they make life convenient and pleasant. They also make for successful living to the degree that they help in the smooth functioning of human relationships.

Many of the proverbs are sayings whose truth is based upon experience. They are observational. Their reliability can be tested by experience. They do not counsel how to act. They simply state the way things are.[5] For example, Proverbs 13:12 tells us, "Hope deferred makes the heart sick, / but a wish fulfilled is a tree of life." This saying is open-ended and subject to verification. It doesn't make a judgment about human conduct. It simply informs the listener about reality, about the truth of things. The statement is simply an affirmation of what experience teaches. Any use or application of this saying is a second move.

The opposite of common sense is foolishness: being silly as opposed to being smart. The fool is one who talks too much (10:8, 19). He utters meaningless words (10:21). He has a warped mind (12:8). His speech is shallow (10:14), "a tale told by an idiot,...signifying nothing," as Shakespeare would describe it. He exercises little restraint (10:19), ready to shoot his mouth off and say whatever comes to mind (13:3). He is "faithless" (11:6), perhaps because he prefers expediency to principle and treats falsehood as good as truth (14:3). Even if corrected, he heeds no rebuke (13:1). He does not realize that words have consequences and that there is a price to pay for the misuse of speech (13:6). He is a simpleton who believes whatever he is told (14:5) and repeats what he hears (11:13). He is so deceived by the sound of his words that he doesn't know where he is going (14:8), but is perverted enough to think that his way seems right in his own eyes (15:7; 12:15). His is the opposite of the shrewd man's wisdom, which "gives him knowledge of his way" (14:8). His thought processes and speech patterns are marred by a lack of common sense. He is heading in the direction of ruin and self-destruction (10:8).

(2) *Moral Integrity.* On a higher plane, proper speech reflects the integrity of good moral conduct: choosing right over wrong, truth over falsehood, justice over wickedness, honesty over dishonesty. Wisdom imitates the order in creation by attempting to bring moral order into our lives.

In contrast to the experiential sayings, which reflect the way things are, the didactic sayings have a distinct moral tone. They contain an ideal, or a value judgment based on a common standard of righteousness.[6] "The just man will never be disturbed, / but the wicked will not abide in the land" (10:30). The wisdom of this saying is practical: it urges us to follow the path of justice and to forsake the path of wickedness. It advocates the view that good moral choices make for wise decisions and bad moral choices make for foolish ones.

Foolishness in being silly is far different from foolishness in being immoral. In the case of silliness, the emphasis was on thoughtlessness and lack of foresight. But in the case of immorality, the emphasis is on intention or motive. It is a question of being evil or wicked in contrast to being good or just. Intentions and considerations of the heart are important (12:5).

Improper speech is the chief enemy of wisdom throughout Proverbs. Words can wound and destroy (12:18) or can offend against propriety and good taste. Speech reveals whether a person has self-control or not. Many proverbs introduce a passional element and distinguish between the "cool" and the "hot" person.[7] The cool person is one who is poised, self-assured, and always self-possessed. The hot person is one who flies off the handle. He cannot control his speech, his desires, his temper, or his rash decision making. He brings harm to others and destroys relations (22:24–25).

A large number of moral infractions gravitate around the key ideals of truth and justice. More weight is given to these two because truth is eternal (12:19) and justice endures (12:3, 12).

Lying and dishonesty can be destructively powerful uses of the tongue (12:17–21). But their gain is short-lived (12:19). "Lying lips are an abomination to the LORD" (12:22). The word *abomination* underscores the fact that lying constitutes a fundamental flaw that affects every other decision. By contrast, truth has an enduring value (12:19). It outlasts dishonesty and deceitfulness. It also brings benefits of peace, security, and joy to one who serves it.

In a similar vein, the plans of those motivated by justice are said to be "legitimate" (12:5). Those who are wicked are "deceitful." The word for *legitimate* means "showing good judgment."[8] The term is borrowed from legal usage, where it concerns the judge rendering a legal decision. The religious meaning is that the upright do what is just in the sense that God accepts them as legally guiltless. On the other hand, the wicked are those who engage in fraud and dishonesty. The Hebrew word for *deceitful* is the same as that used for false scales (11:1).[9] Legally the guilty will be condemned for concrete acts of fraud. There was a time when lying in the presence of the king was considered treacherous. The person caught lying would have his tongue cut off (10:31). Such a person could never be trusted.

There is an epitaph that an Egyptian noble left on his tomb. It said: "SILENT, COOL IN TEMPERAMENT, CALM IN EXPRESSION!"[10] It summed up the ideal scribe and statesman for Egypt. The wicked were thought to be "hot under the collar," capable of violence and treachery, which, if not brought under control, could result in the city being overthrown (11:11).

Traditional wisdom, which has been well tested, seems to favor a person of cool temper. It even sings his praises: "A patient man is better than a warrior, / and he who rules his temper, than he who takes a city" (16:32).

(3) *Obedience to God.* Most of all, speech must reflect obedience to God's law, the Torah, God's book of sacred instruction. Speech that is steeped in wisdom must mirror a life lived in covenant relationship to Yahweh, the source of all wisdom (8:1–36).

Mindfulness of Yahweh and his teachings should penetrate every aspect of our life, including even secular wisdom. This outlook is preserved in the phrase "the fear of the LORD." It is the foundational principle of all wisdom in Proverbs and forms an inclusion to the entire work.

The idea that God must guide the beginning, the middle, and the end of all discourse is crucial to the Hebrew ideal of wisdom. Even in the secular proverbs contained in the middle section of the book (10:1—22:16), the intrusion of Yahweh's name occurs many times in 14:16—16:15. This is done deliberately for two reasons.

The first is *theological* and is intended to show that true wisdom, even secular wisdom, can never exist without God: "Man may make plans in his heart, / but what the tongue utters is from the LORD" (16:1). We might think that the cleverest utterance that spontaneously springs from our mouth is evidence of our own human endowment. That may well be, but only because God gave us that endowment in the first place. To remind us of this, Proverbs gives us this admonition: "Entrust your works to the LORD, / and your plans will succeed" (16:3).

The second reason is *structural.* The wisdom teacher who did the final editing had in his hands two separate collections entitled "Proverbs of Solomon." The first collection (10:1—15:33) was marked predominantly by antithetic parallelism. The second collection (16:1—22:16) was characterized predominantly by synonymous parallelism. The editor sewed these two collections together by inserting some "Yahweh sayings" in the middle, bringing the total collection of sayings to 375.[11] This is the numerical value of the Hebrew name for Solomon *(slmh).* The wisdom teacher wanted to remind us that the gift of wisdom that Solomon received from God was at work in every aspect of Solomon's life. So must it be in ours if wisdom is not to go awry, as it sometimes does.

Wisdom's Third Fall from Grace: The Tripping Tongue

When fortune favors us and all is going well, we see wisdom at work. But that may also be the time when we are most vulnerable and neglect to take care of those less fortunate out of our abundant resources. We may even be the cause of their misfortune. So Proverbs reminds us of our responsibility by offering a negative admonition: "Injure not the poor because they are poor, / nor crush the needy at the gate; / For the LORD will defend their cause, / and will plunder the lives of those who plunder them" (22:22–23).

The road to folly is clearly marked. When our intellect is dimmed to the point that common sense escapes us, we say and do silly things. When our will is weak, the lure of what is evil suddenly becomes attractive. When our spirit loses the sense of God, then even the creatures that reveal his presence become our partners in crime.

Where Are All the Speech Writers?

Proverbs are a veritable gold mine for speech writers. Besides being a collection of wisdom sayings, they are also brilliant literary gems. They exploit the speech writer's craft for making every word tell. By reason of their content, structure, form, and style, they serve as models for good writing and excellent speech making.

Content: Proverbial sayings contain wisdom for every age and for almost every occasion. They are valuable resources for a toastmaster. Many of them are commonsense observations whose truths have stood the test of time. What parent has not found it necessary on occasion to use punishment with moderation according to Proverbs 19:18: "Chastise your son, for in this there is hope; / but do not desire his death"? Other proverbs promote moral values that strengthen the fabric of society. "Many are declared to be men of virtue: / but who can find one worthy of trust?" (20:6). Still others come packaged with deep spiritual insights that elevate and transform human existence: "All the ways of a man may be right in his own eyes, / but it is the LORD who proves hearts" (21:2). A speech writer who has such precious gems at his fingertips will find in them much inspiration.

Structure. Proverbs also suggest a basic structural design, without which a writer's speech has nowhere to go. A writer waiting to be inspired finds in proverbs a premise with which to begin a discourse, or a conclusion with which to successfully terminate one. A proverb is a miniature speech. In the hands of a skillful writer, it can easily be expanded into a larger, coherent discourse. Design is basic to any speech. It lets the writer know where he or she is heading and how to get there. A proverb is a story waiting to be told. It readily suggests a transitional or topical sentence to build upon.

Form. Proverbs are, in addition, excellent literary gems. We will have more to say about this when we deal with patterns of proverbs. For now let us just note that they are carefully crafted so as to elicit the appropriate emotion or response. They are deceptively simple yet surprisingly profound. They are compellingly persuasive and delightfully pleasing.

Rhythm, sound, and sense conspire "to ignite a certain combination of words, causing them to explode in the mind."[12]

Whatever the art form that clothes the proverb, be it assonance, alliteration, or parallelism, it never becomes a mannerism. There is enough variation to prevent the dullness of repetition.

Most of the proverbs are written in parallel form. Parallel construction is effective for expressing similar ideas. Likeness of form enables the listener to recognize likeness of content or function. In the wisdom schools this form was used to carry out the activity of teaching and learning: a cue-and-response technique for making education a partnership enterprise, with room for creativity and inspiration.

Style. Finally, proverbs are models of style. Every writer knows that the surest way to arouse and hold the attention of a listener or reader is to be specific, definite, and concrete. Proverbs are all of these. They are vigorous and concise. They omit nothing and say everything that needs to be said. They contain no unnecessary words, so they hold together as a compact unit. They make every word tell.

These terse, compact wisdom sayings illustrate what every experienced writer knows: It is better to use fewer words to express one's thoughts than many. Expressing thought in a positive rather than a negative manner makes language vigorous and strong instead of weak and limp. Active verbs, for the most part, make for greater clarity than passive verbs. Using too many qualifiers and unnecessary parenthetical phrases diminishes the force of speech and is detrimental to good writing.

Every writer aspires to become immortal, to make his mark on history, to be remembered by generations to come. Proverbs use words in such a way as to show durability. They never grow stale. They last.

Most of all, proverbs contain enviable qualities of inspiration and creativity to which every writer aspires. Words, those most intimate expressions of a person's inner thought, are directed to effects never dreamed of by the speaker (16:1–3). A man's tongue may be the rudder that steers his speech in the direction he wishes it to take. But when, in a moment of sheer inspiration, he manages to capture the desired emotion, he has the uncanny feeling that someone else is the pilot (cf. 16:9). Ultimately every writer knows that the best of human endeavor is naught unless it is animated by a wisdom not entirely of this earth. If he is honest, he must ask himself this question: why do words expressed in a certain way have the power to stir the listener deeply, while the same words, slightly rearranged, leave him cold and untouched? Expressed in a certain way, they communicate overpowering emotion. What might otherwise be prosy and wooden becomes poetical and sensuous.

Wisdom, in Proverbs, is forthright in reminding us that there is something divine in human inspiration. Even though she comes disguised as a woman (1:20–33; 8:22–31), she is quick to remind her clients of her divine origin. She speaks with the prophetic voice of authority. By her ubiquitous presence she lures the simple to seek wisdom. Whoever surrenders to her designs soon learns to communicate her secrets creatively. They become adept at revealing new insights or new applications of older insights to new situations. When wisdom animates human speech, it blossoms forth into a form of creative communication.

A soul set on the edge of eternity receives the power to shed new light on our human way of seeing things. It is as if the truth of things, so long hidden, suddenly becomes revealed. A moment of inspiration is truly a gift by which, in the words of Francis Thompson, "we touch but a stone and start a wing."[13]

Chapter 13

If You Can Mix with Kings and Yet Not Lose the Common Touch!

Wisdom was formerly reserved for kings and members of the royal court. Now it is offered to all. It raises the most common among us and makes us fit to dine at the king's banqueting table.

---

1. Wisdom Is a Princely Art, but It Is Offered to All

In ancient Middle Eastern countries, wisdom education was reserved for the elite. Wisdom teachers were called in to instruct the children of the royal household. Wisdom schools were established for the education of scribes as well as for the officials of the royal court. One of King Solomon's greatest achievements was to establish wisdom schools in Israel after the Egyptian model; but instead of wisdom being reserved only for the privileged few, it was to be made available to all. The book of Proverbs was one of the products of the scribal schools King Solomon had established. By giving parents and teachers the opportunity to use

Proverbs 22:11 *'Winning speech' catches the ear of the King and even of Yahweh himself.*

these materials for instructing their children and students, it was hoped that these in turn would become a kingly people.

Kings. Proverbs are addressed primarily to kings. They have a special bond with God and with the people they serve. The king enjoys a special relation to God as "son" and as his "anointed" (Ps 2:7; 72:1). This was particularly true of King David because his heart was always turned toward God. Through the example of this shepherd boy who became king, the king also came to be looked upon as "shepherd" of God's people (Exod 34:23). In view of this double relationship, the king must embody the divine concern for justice. As God's emissary, he endeavors to bring about God's reign on earth.

Proverbs underscores some of the privileges that flow from this relationship. The king's words share divine authority. As long as he abides in covenant relationship to Yahweh, inspired decisions will be on his lips and his mouth will not sin in judgment (16:10). He will uphold the order of both justice and right judgment (21:3). He will acknowledge Yahweh's direct control over every aspect of life and human planning, and even wisdom itself (16:1–7), as David did. He will endeavor to establish a rule of righteousness by which his throne endures (16:12). By avoiding wrongdoing, he will be assured of the wise guidance that descends from above.

Ideally, the king is a symbol of wisdom. He embodies a healthy combination of common sense, virtue, and spiritual insight. His own ingenuity (21:2), strengthened by a sense for what is right and just (21:3), and his openness to divine guidance (21:1) make him an object of both love and fear. His presence creates an atmosphere that attracts wise conduct and repels foolish behavior (20:8, 28). At the same time, "A wise king winnows the wicked, / and threshes them under the cart-wheel" (20:26). Ultimately the wisdom by which kings rule is more a work of grace than an ingrained natural endowment: "Like a stream is the king's heart in the hand of the LORD; / wherever it pleases him, he directs it" (21:1). The metaphor of irrigation comes to mind. The irrigator has full control over the water supply; so also God over his earthly representative.

The People. The same is true of the people he serves: "All the ways of a man may be right in his own eyes, / but it is the LORD who proves hearts." (21:2). Kings and people share a common

116

bond. One is incomplete without the other. Proverbs 14:28 states: "In many subjects lies the glory of the king; / but if his people are few, it is the prince's ruin." To those who live in the aura of the king's presence, wisdom becomes contagious: "He who pursues justice and kindness / will find life and honor" (21:21). "There is no wisdom, no understanding, / no counsel against the LORD" (21:30).

No kingdom can be established in the divine order of righteousness unless the people also live by the same qualities as kings. Their submissiveness to the king to gain his favor is an extension of the king's submissiveness to Yahweh. When kings and people alike observe the order of divine justice, then clearly wisdom flows from God through the king to the people. Within this framework of a well-ordered system of government, based on justice, the king is simply the conduit through which divine wisdom descends and becomes incarnate in God's people. Only then can "the light of the king's countenance" symbolize life and his favor resemble "a rain cloud in spring" (16:15). Seeking the king's favor and catering to his wishes is less of a fawning gesture and more of an observance of a divine order and an attempt to please God himself. Fearing God and fearing the king are put on the same level in 24:21.

Subservience, rightly understood, is the foundation for acquiring the kingly qualities of "good sense" (16:22) and "pleasing speech" (16:21). It helps make one "humble with the meek" rather than "share plunder with the proud" (16:19). The excoriation of evil words (16:27–30), coupled with respect for elders

(16:31) and a cool temper (16:32), is part and parcel of the wisdom that is distinctive of the royal court.

It is always possible for those of lowly estate to win the king's favor. If they have the right mix of character and pleasing qualities, they might even advance to a high position: "The LORD loves the pure of heart; / the man of winning speech has the king for his friend" (22:11). In Middle Eastern countries it was customary for kings to choose a very special person for a friend. He would have access to the king's garden. There he could help the king relax and engage him in pleasing conversation. Anyone with unusual skill and proper behavior could go far in the royal bureaucracy (22:29). Sitting to dine with the king requires that one observe proper decorum and humility. It could be a step to advancement in the king's favor (23:1–3). Training in etiquette and good manners was part of the curriculum of wisdom teaching. They were socially acknowledged marks of good breeding.

Proverbs 22:9 suggests a connection between a king and kindness. Kindness, especially toward the poor, is an effective way of establishing kinship ties with them. It attracts divine blessings. The king is a tower of strength to the poor and the oppressed, especially since they have no one to defend them (23:10–11). The kingly virtue of being "zealous for the rights of the poor" (29:14) is an aspect of justice. "By justice a king gives stability to the land" (29:4). A king who rules with justice reflects the enduring value of wisdom as well as the permanence and stability of the divine order. Protecting the poor not only attracts divine blessings (29:13); it is also a way of making sure that there will be no dissidents that will threaten his rule.

If You Can Mix with Kings...

The kingly art of wisdom, once reserved for the royal elite, is now available to all. In wisdom literature, kingship is a metaphor for wisdom. The king plays an important role as intermediary between divine and human wisdom. By election and vocation, he comes endowed with the ability to serve the best interests of his people. As wisdom becomes an ingrained gift, the people become a kingly people.

When king and people alike are fully surrendered to God, they are assured of a life of peace, prosperity, and security: "When the LORD is pleased with a man's ways, / he makes even his enemies be at peace with him" (16:7). David was a man after God's heart. God gave him victory in battle over his enemies. Solomon asked for and received the gift of wisdom. His reign was marked by universal peace and prosperity, with kings and princes paying tribute to him. Solomon, more than David, illustrates that wisdom is mightier than military prowess (24:5–6). David is the strong hero, Solomon the wise ruler. Yahweh is the model for both (see Isa 31:2; Jer 10:12; 51:15; Dan 2:20; Ps 147:5; Job 26:12). Even though wisdom guides the hand that secures victory in war, as David did, wisdom is superior to strength.

In the end, there are three things a king most needs: a pure heart, a clear mind, and a just spirit (cf. 31:3–9). The first protects the wisdom he has gained through much labor. The second helps to discover what is right. The third helps secure the reign of justice.

2. Riding the Wisdom Train Are Hezekiah's Men; but Who Are These Foreign Kings?

King Hezekiah's reign (715–687 B.C.E.) illustrates the dilemma of wisdom: should we listen to the voices of human wisdom, or should we seek the wisdom that comes from God? There need be no conflict between the two, since human wisdom is the cultivation of our natural human endowment, which itself is a gift of God. On the other hand, the horizon of human wisdom is limited. It can sometimes go awry. Proverbs 3:5 therefore counsels us "Trust in the LORD with all your heart, / on your own intelligence rely not." And again: "Be not wise in your own eyes" (3:7). In many ways Hezekiah reminds us of King Solomon.

Hezekiah's Men

Hezekiah was the first Judean king since Solomon to reign without a rival king of northern Israel. This gave him the opportunity to bring together the historical and religious writings of the two peoples, including wisdom materials.

Like King Solomon, Hezekiah gave a great impetus to the wisdom movement. "The men of Hezekiah" mentioned in 25:1 are members of a school or scribal establishment under Hezekiah's royal patronage. The title reminds us that, in addition to the proverbs of 10:1—22:16, other proverbs that were attributed to Solomon existed in written or oral form. Hezekiah's men were busy assembling, revising, copying, and transmitting this material, which had become available to them. Two hundred years later the wisdom movement was continuing in full strength.

According to 2 Chronicles 29–32, Hezekiah fostered a national revival with Solomon as his model. He suppressed the local shrines that threatened Israel's faith. He purified Judah's worship, removing the Assyrian altar that had been installed in the temple. Lastly, he centralized Judah's worship in the temple at Jerusalem. Because of this wholesale national revival, the Deuteronomic editor in 2 Kings 18 gave unqualified approval to Hezekiah's reign. He compared him to King David: "and neither before him nor after him was there anyone like him among all the kings of Judah" (2 Kgs 18:5). This tribute was based on the premise that the true worship of Yahweh must be centralized in Jerusalem. These reforms brought Hezekiah into direct confrontation with Assyria.

There were conspiracies in the east, instigated by Babylon, and in the west, instigated by Egypt. Hezekiah threw in his lot with the conspirators, no doubt under the advice of his counselors. On the basis of astute human calculation, it seemed the best course of action to take. But Isaiah, led by a higher wisdom from Yahweh, warned Hezekiah to stay out of the conspiracy (Isa 20). Hezekiah did not listen. Sennacherib came with lightning speed, destroyed many of Judah's cities, and laid siege to Jerusalem.

Hezekiah turned to Egypt. As in the days of Solomon, the ruling circles of Jerusalem were in close contact with Egypt and under a strong Egyptian political and cultural influence (cf. Isa 29:13–16, 30:1–7; 31:1–3). They counted on Pharaoh's support against an Assyrian invasion. Egypt at this time was ruled by an Ethiopian king, Shabako by name, who headed the twenty-fifth dynasty.[1] Once again Isaiah denounced those who went down to Egypt for help, trusting "in chariots because of their number, and in horsemen because of their combined power" (31:1–3). Proverbs 21:31 supports this view: "The horse is equipped for the day of battle, / but the victory is the LORD's." Egypt was defeated, and Ethiopia taken into exile. Hezekiah realized that the wise men of Judah and of Egypt had both been wrong.

So now he turned to Yahweh and sought Isaiah's counsel. The "wise men" of the court with their calculated pro-Egyptian policy had failed because of their distrust in Yahweh. "Yet he too [Yahweh] is wise," Isaiah could remind them (Isa 31:2). With Sennacherib's soldiers surrounding Jerusalem, Hezekiah was like a bird in a cage. In this extremity Isaiah's counsel was like a breath of fresh air: "By waiting and by calm you shall be saved, / in quiet and in trust your strength lies" (30:15). Here Isaiah is giving Hezekiah a summary of the meaning of faith. The result is staggering: when Yahweh has finished all his work on Mount Zion and in Jerusalem, he will "punish the utterance / of the king of Assyria's proud heart" (Isa 10:12). Sennacherib called off the siege and returned home. Yahweh is the king. Earthly rulers are but his instruments to carry out his purposes. True wisdom wins out in the end, even over military might.

Hezekiah had learned his lesson: "God has glory in what he conceals, / kings have glory in what they fathom" (25:2). Yahweh invests kings with enough wisdom to rule over their subjects. But ultimately God's wisdom rules over all creation. It is unassailable and is the guarantee of all earthly wisdom. Human wisdom is good, and its guidance is reliable for the most part. Divine wisdom is better. No amount of human astuteness must be allowed to blur the distinction. By seeking Yahweh's guidance in all our decisions, we can prevent human wisdom from leading us astray. In the end, Hezekiah's trust in Yahweh secured better results than his trust in his counselors.

Foreign Kings

In the segments immediately before and after the second collection of Solomonic proverbs, we come across veiled or explicit references to foreign sources, which the Hebrew editor used to make up the remaining proverbs in the book. The two veiled sources are Amen-em-Ope and Ahiquar; Agur and Lemuel are explicitly mentioned. They are not royal personages, but they do have a royal message. We find each of them giving kingly advice to a son or official of a royal court or to citizens of the upper class. In each case the advice is centered on how to get on in life, how to be successful.

Amen-em-Ope. Proverbs 22:17—24:22 consists of a collection of thirty sayings. There are striking similarities in content between Proverbs 22:17—23:11 and a seventh-century Egyptian work known as *The Instruction of Amen-em-Ope.* This work was also divided into thirty chapters, or "houses." Because of these coincidences, the New American Bible has amended a corrupt text to make explicit these references: "I make known to you the words of Amen-em-Ope. / Have I not written for you the "Thirty," / with counsels and knowledge" (22:19–20).[2]

Amen-em-Ope styles himself a scribe who renders a variety of services to his master who happens to be a king. He wishes to pass on his legacy of wisdom to his son, his followers, and a host of upper-class citizens like himself. He gives practical advice on not mistreating the poor, on avoiding the hot-tempered person, on showing proper respect when in the presence of the king, and on not letting wealth get in the way.[3] There is a special reference to a skilled craftsman in Proverbs 22:29. Such a one, we are told, will attract the king's notice. While competence in a particular trade or profession constitutes a special kind of wisdom, the Egyptian text has in mind the profession of the scribe. He is the one who is skilled in words. He knows how to make speech elegant and pleasing. Such a one will go far in the king's service.

The Hebrew scribe did not merely copy sayings from an outside source. He adapted them to his own Jewish cultural heritage and religious tradition. His purpose in incorporating these sayings is not merely to advance in life. His stated purpose is this: "That your trust may be in the LORD" (22:19). Whatever wisdom teaches us is the right thing to do must be measured by the extent to which our human endeavor conforms to the divine will. The Hebrew scribe who compiled these sayings gives two instances where trust in Yahweh is violated. The first concerns one who does evil—for example by robbing the poor. Amen-em-Ope says that the floodwaters, the north wind, the thunder will find him. Eventually the moon god (Thoth) will establish his guilt. He cannot escape.[4] The Hebrew author says plainly that the poor will have the Lord to defend them. The failure of wisdom is also a failure of our covenanted relation with Yahweh.

A second instance concerns dispossessing orphans of their land by changing the landmarks. Amen-em-Ope does recognize that such an offense is a violation of the god's will. In Israelite tradition Yahweh is the "redeemer" of the helpless (Prov 23:11; see also 19:17, 21:13; 22:9).

Ahiquar. Proverbs 23:12 is another standard formula for introducing the wisdom instruction form, like 22:17. Only this time it points to a new source: *The Words of Ahiquar.*[5] The sayings that follow are similar to those of Ahiquar. A copy of this work was found in the remains of a fifth-century B.C.E. Jewish colony at Elephantine in Upper Egypt. From his own introductory remarks, Ahiquar seems to have exerted much influence at the royal courts of Sennacherib (704-681 B.C.E.) and Esarhaddon (680-669 B.C.E.). The work was very popular among the Jews.

Once again the Hebrew author does not simply copy sayings but shows great originality in the way he integrates them into the Jewish tradition. Notice how he stresses the family as the source of wisdom in Proverbs 23:22–23. This is sometimes called "clan wisdom" because it is passed on by parents and elders rather than in the scribal schools (23:15–24). At the time Proverbs was being compiled, the Jews were strongly drawn to Egyptian wisdom. The Hebrew wisdom teacher reminds them that the wisdom their parents taught them would give them a future with hope because is was steeped in zeal "for the fear of the LORD always" (23:17–18). The blessings that Yahweh attaches to our obedience will endure forever. For this reason the wisdom teacher makes a passionate appeal to the Jews to gladden their parents by speaking what is right (23:15–16). Notice the artistic arrangement of these two verses in a chiasm: *your—my:my—your.* This arrangement is made obvious in the Anchor Bible version: "My son, if *your* mind be wise, *my* own mind will be content; *my* innermost being will rejoice when *your* lips speak what is right."

Agur. Proverbs 30:1–6 introduces us to "The words of Agur." All we know of him is that he came from Massa, the home of an Ishmaelite people of northern Arabia. The opening statement, though couched in the words of a skeptic, is indirectly an inverse way of stating one's belief, or at least one's desire to know God.

The pretensions of wisdom to know all there is to know are challenged by such ultimate questions the skeptic raises: "Who has gone up to heaven and come down again— / who has cupped the wind in his hands? / Who has bound up the waters in a cloak— / who has marked out all the ends of the earth? / What is his name, what is his son's name, / if you know it?" (30:4). The true skeptic in each of us must be humbled in the face of such questions. There is not enough wisdom in all the world to comprehend who God is. For all our intelligence, we simply must bow to the fact that God is beyond our capacity to grasp him. No one can completely master wisdom because wisdom is with God. We lack wisdom inasmuch as we lack knowledge of God and of God's infinite designs.

Yet Israel, of all nations, had come to know God in a unique way. He was not just a god among other gods, nor even just a god above other gods. Israel's God always was, always is, and always will be the one and only true God, before whom no other god exists and to whom all others must bow. When Israel borrows the wisdom common to other nations, it integrates this wisdom into the unique notion of God. This is what makes Israel's wisdom a revelation. So, when we read the wisdom sayings, we are not receiving merely secular advice. We are trying to bring order into every aspect of our lives in the light of our unique relation to Yahweh. That is what makes Israel's wisdom tradition unique and radically different from all other wisdom traditions.

God's word is eternal; human words fade away. Agur's initial skepticism gives way to belief: "Every word of God is tested; / he is a shield to those who take refuge in him" (30:5). Agur stands in awe before the mystery of God's transcendence. God's word is always to be trusted and stands without any need of help from any of us. In the following two verses he prays that God may guard him from a lying tongue and from want so he may not be tempted to deny God or to cease trusting in his loving care. What a prayer from a skeptic! In many ways Agur reminds us of Job.

There is a double meaning in the word *Massa*. As a place of origin, it was the home of the Edomites. Edom was reputed for its wisdom (see Jer 49:7; Obad 8). The word also means "an oracle." Agur's "pronouncement of mortal man" turns out to be a prophetic oracle from God. Like Amen-em-Ope (Prov 22:17) and Ahiquar (23:12), Agur had a listening heart. It was there, in the intimacy of his innermost being, that the true skeptic became also the true believer. He had the wisdom to know that the wisdom he possessed was insufficient. His humility was blessed: he received the wisdom he claimed not to have. It was to know the one and only true God.

Lemuel. No such person is known to have existed by this name. He might be just anybody, or even a nobody. It doesn't really matter. The person of Lemuel is a "king fiction" to lend authority to the advice given. For a man of his status, he is described in the Anchor Bible version as one who "acted foolishly" (Prov 31:1, 4). The queen mother exercises her prerogative to reproach him for his foolishness and to admonish him of his kingly duty.

Lemuel is assigned the same place of origin as Agur. The New American Bible plays on the double meaning of *Massa*. It is the place name for where Lemuel happens to be king. At the same time it also means "advice," thus aptly recalling the advice given by the queen mother to the king-to-be. The urgency of her admonition is signaled by the repetition of the word *What* three times. She warns her son against the three dangers to which kings were most often exposed: women, wine, and disregard of the needy and the oppressed. Wisdom's cause will best be served by purity, temperance, and the administration of justice toward the defenseless. These are wisdom's three prerequisites for kings: a pure heart, a clear mind, and a just spirit (31:1–9).

In Middle Eastern countries, kings were perceived to wield much power. They often did what they pleased. For this reason they were often feared. Evildoers would tremble in the presence of the king for the judgment that was coming to them. Even good people who happened to be poor, or oppressed, or in any way wronged stood in mortal awe of the king. A striking example is that of Naboth, who lost his vineyard to the evil king Ahab through the wiles of the king's wife, Jezebel (1 Kings 21). The wisdom in Proverbs reminds us to "fear the LORD and the king" (24:21). If we can be afraid of kings, how much more afraid we should be of the judgment and punishment of God!

Chapter 14

Now Let's All Have a Little Fun! Patterns of Proverbs: A Lesson in Literary Taste

---

Proverbs are nuggets of wisdom clothed in beautiful art forms, designed to make them pleasing and the wisdom they contain desirable. One can hardly imagine the intense literary activity that helped make the exchange between teacher and pupil a fun-loving enterprise.

The heart of the proverb is a comparison. Out of this grew a variety of patterns:
Simple, Double, and Triple Comparisons;
Varying Forms of Identity, Similarity, and Value;
Varying Forms of Contrast, including What Is Contrary to Right Order (such as the Mocking Comparison, the Rhetorical Question, the Absurd);
Forms of Classification or Characterization (including Numerical Proverbs and the Characterization of Persons, Actions, or Situations);
Proverbs of Consequence;

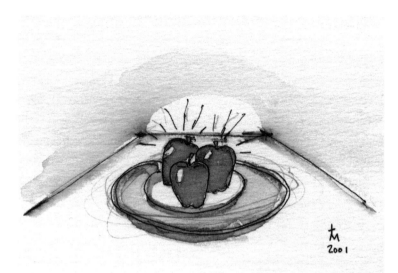

Proverbs 25:11 *"Like golden apples in silver settings are words spoken at the proper time."*

Other Poetic Devices (such as Riddle and Answer, Hyperbole, Fable, Irony, Alliteration, Pun, Personification, Parable);

Various Forms of Arrangements (such as Chiasm, Acrostic, Inclusion);

Forms of Parallelism (Synonymous, Antithetic, Synthetic).

All these, and many other art forms, went a long way toward making the pupil a true "craftsman of speech." They also contributed toward making proverbial wisdom a gold mine for speech writers, speech makers, and those wanting to try out their literary skills.

Now Let's All Have a Little Fun!

The Play Way of Education in Proverbs

As tools for educational instruction, proverbs proved to be popular and fun-loving ways of teaching and learning wisdom. The cue-and-response technique used in the wisdom schools served as a contest of wits between teacher and pupil.[1] It was fun. It sparked up interest on both sides. There was rapport between teacher and pupil. It created a healthy atmosphere for learning. Many of the proverbs were an outcome of this contest: part was provided by the teacher and part by the pupil. There was much creativity and possibly even laughter, which must have animated the learning process.

Even the terse, vigorous style and striking imagery of the proverbs made them pleasant to the ear and also easy to remember. They gave the young trainees ready access to the ancestral wisdom of the past. But they were also literary devices for stimulating creativity in thought and expression and for discovering new ways to apply the wisdom learned to changing conditions.[2] We can hardly imagine the enormous outpouring of literary activity that surrounded the copying, recitation, and compiling of proverbs.

There was a common pool of wisdom sayings, many dating back to antiquity. Sumeria, Assyria, Babylonia, and Egypt had each their own collections. So did Israel and its immediate neighbors. By the time of King Solomon, we find the wisdom teachers of Israel observing, classifying, reflecting, making comparisons and analogies, and finally drawing conclusions for daily living. Out of this prodigious activity was born the final edition of Proverbs as we have it today.

The sages were not content with merely preserving the collection of wisdom sayings for posterity, even though that in itself

131

would have been of great value. They went further: they paid close attention not only to what was being said (the content of the proverb) but also to the manner in which it was said (the form). They went to great pains in crafting the proverb into a highly sophisticated art form. The proverbs reveal certain distinguishable patterns.

Patterns of Proverbs

Comparison

The most obvious meaning of the Hebrew word for proverb *(mashal)* is "a comparison." The sages often looked for comparisons in nature in order to draw lessons for human behavior. The author of the proverb tries to exhibit the real nature of human behavior by comparing it to something else.

A. *Simple Comparison:* "Like golden apples in silver settings / are words spoken at the proper time" (Prov 25:11). Seeing apples beautifully arranged in a silver-tray setting reminds the author of the appropriateness of the seasonal word.

B. *Double and Triple Comparisons:* Examples of similes that include double or triple comparisons are 25:12; 25:20; 25:26; and 26:3. Sometimes a tone of stinging sarcasm accompanies the comparison, as in the case of a sluggard who sets one's teeth on edge like vinegar or blinds the eyes like smoke (10:26).

C. *Identity:* At times the comparison takes the form of identity, equivalence, or invariable association.[3] The identity in question can be expressed in various ways:

(1) "This is really (or always) that." As in 29:5: "The man who flatters his neighbor / is spreading a net under his feet." One can be lured into the same web of deceitfulness that one plans for others.

(2) "Where (or when) this is, that is." As in 16:7: "When the LORD is pleased with a man's ways, / he makes even his enemies be at peace with him." One can hardly escape the fact that this proverb aptly reflects the situation of King Solomon.

(3) "Without this, there is no that." As in 14:4 AB: "Without (the labor of) oxen, the manger is bare." This translation also carries the commentary that "this is an analogical adage on human behavior." A similar sentiment is expressed in 2 Thessalonians 3:10.

D. *Similarity:* Underlying a comparison is sometimes the notion of similarity, analogy, or type. Here again, similarity can be expressed in different ways:

(1) "This is (or acts like) that." As in 25:28: "Like an open city with no defenses / is the man with no check on his feelings." The original Hebrew has the word *ruah* ("spirit") instead of "feelings." The meaning is clear: Evil will readily overcome the person whose spirit has not been trained in the moderation and self-control proposed by the wisdom teachers.

(2) "As this, so that." As in 25:19: "Like an infected tooth or an unsteady foot / is (dependence on) a faithless man in time of trouble." His unreliability stems from the fact that he lacks the

moderation and self-control recommended for the wise in 25:6–16.

(3) "This is (metaphorically) that." As in 12:4: "A worthy wife is the crown of her husband." Other examples: "The king's lips are an oracle" (16:10); "The fruit of virtue is a tree of life" (11:30). (The tree of life is a metaphor for health and long life; the idea is derived from Gen 2:9; 3:22. Sirach pictures wisdom as a rich and beautiful fruit tree [24:12–17].)

E. *Value:* Some proverbs of comparison carry the notion of value, relative value, priority, proportion, or degree. They can be expressed in many forms:

(1) "This is worth that." As in 22:1: "A good name is more desirable than great riches." Riches perish, but the memory of a good man endures even after his death.

(2) "The more (or less) this, the more (or less) that." As in 21:27: "The sacrifice of the wicked is an abomination, / the more so when they offer it with a bad intention."

(3) "Better this than that." This class of proverbs is known as "better than" proverbs. An example is 19:22: "Rather be a poor man than a liar."

(4) "First this, then that." As in 22:10: "Expel the arrogant man and discord goes out; / strife and insult cease."

(5) "This in proportion to that." In 24:13–14 we read that wisdom is to the soul what honey is to the palate. Honey is used as a favorite sweetener in Near Eastern countries. Even today, stores throughout the Arab world are filled with pastries smothered in honey. It is a very high tribute to wisdom to think of it as honey to the soul.

(6) "If this, how much more that!" As in 11:31: "If the just man is punished on earth, / how much more the wicked and the sinner!"

Contrast

A second category of patterns is the opposite of a comparison. It points to nonidentity, contrast, or paradox.

A. *Simple Contrast:*

(1) "This is not really that." As in 25:15: "A soft tongue will break a bone." The sharp contrast between soft and hard heightens our curiosity as to how something so delicate and fragile as a "soft word" can overcome something so obdurate as a "hardened heart." "Bone" could possibly be a metaphor for a person's impenetrable and unchangeable hard feelings.

(2) "Not every this is that." Proverbs 20:6 can be reworded thus: "Not all who are declared to be men of virtue are found to be worthy of trust." As one commentator observes, a person may seem virtuous enough when he makes fair promises, but he may fail the test in carrying them out faithfully.[4]

(3) "This is paradoxically that." As in 27:7: "but to the man who is hungry, any bitter thing is sweet."

B. *What Is Contrary to Right Order,* and therefore futile or absurd:

(1) The mocking comparison. For example, a favorite sarcasm about early risers is 26:14: "The door turns on its hinges, / the sluggard, on his bed!"

(2) The rhetorical question. A teacher of privileged youth reflects ruefully: "Of what use in the fool's hand are the means / to buy wisdom, since he has no mind for it?" (17:16). After all, money cannot buy wisdom if one has neither the desire nor the discipline for acquiring it.

(3) Futility or absurdity. Another teacher, an instructor of wisdom, clinches his warning of the dire consequences of associating with thieves by quoting the proverb "It is in vain that a net is spread / before the eyes of any bird" (1:17).

Classification or Characterization

A. *Classification:* An example of classification is 26:3. It puts the horse, the donkey, and the fool in the same category. They all need a beating to be brought under control.

B. *Numerical Proverbs of Classification:* The most famous of several examples quoted in 30:15–30 is: "Three things are too wonderful for me, / yes, four I cannot understand: / The way of an eagle in the air, / the way of a serpent upon a rock, / The way of a ship on the high seas, / and the way of a man with a maiden" (30:18–19). The dynamics of a numerical proverb will be discussed in a later section.

C. *Progressive Classification:* An example is found in 27:3: "Stone is heavy, and sand a burden, / but a fool's provocation is heavier than both."

D. *Characterization of Persons, Actions, or Situations.* Proverbs affords many examples of such characterizations:
(1) *The fool* —"The simpleton believes everything"(14:15).
(2) *The scoffer* —"but the senseless one heeds no rebuke" (13:1).
(3) *The sluggard* —"The sluggard loses his hand in the dish; / he is too weary to lift it to his mouth" (26:15).
(4) *The shrewish wife*—"and the nagging of a wife is a persistent leak." (19:13).

Proverbs of Consequence

A proverb of consequence is intended to illustrate how words or actions carry within them the power to bring good or harm to others. Examples of such proverbs are "A glad heart lights up the face" (15:13); "He who digs a pit falls into it" (26:27); "In seedtime the sluggard plows not; / when he looks for the harvest, it is not there" (20:4). Such proverbs figure prominently, especially in the instruction genre of wisdom teaching. The teacher tries to give a graphic picture of where a certain action or speech or thought is likely to lead in order to deter his pupils from heading in this dangerous direction.

Other Poetic Devices Used for Effect

A. *Riddle and Answer:* This was a favorite genre of folk wisdom. Solomon's success in solving the riddles put to him by the queen of Sheba is well known (1 Kgs 10:1–3). As a contest of wits, riddles were often used as a form of entertainment.

Sometimes the answer might be given in the form of a riddle. This would be the case when the contestants were equally well matched. But most often the riddle was given by one party, usually the teacher, leaving the pupil to figure out the answer. If the pupil were slow to come up with an appropriate response, the teacher himself might oblige by filling in a possible answer himself. If the answer seemed fitting, he might get a nod of approval or a smile. In the context of education, the goal would almost always be the edification of the pupil. Proverbs 23:29–35 provides a good illustration:

(1) *The Riddle* (posed by the teacher):
   Who scream? Who shriek?
   Who have strife? Who have anxiety?
   Who have wounds for nothing?
   Who have black eyes?
(2) *The Answer* (given by one or more pupils):
   Those who linger long over wine,
   those who engage in trials of blended wine.

(3) *Justification:* (assuming that these might be two similar but different responses from two of his more brilliant pupils, the teacher could not miss the opportunity of rewarding them by dramatizing his justification):

   Look not on the wine when it is red,
   when it sparkles in the glass.
   It goes down smoothly;
   but in the end it bites like a serpent,
   or like a poisonous adder.

Your eyes behold strange sights,
and your heart utters disordered thoughts;
You are like one now lying in the depths of the sea
now sprawled at the top of the mast.
"They struck me, but it pained me not;
They beat me, but I felt it not;
When shall I awake
to seek wine once again?"

The teacher paints a graphic picture of the evils of alcohol. The opening and closing verses describe the effects of heavy drinking. The image of the biting of a snake suggests its fatal results: distorted vision or fancies, incoherent or irresponsible speech, warbly or unbalanced gait, insensitivity to pain, and the half-stupid assurances of returning consciousness.

B. *Hyperbole:* A form of exaggeration to create a desired effect, as in 2:18. The proverb emphasizes the fate of the faithless wife: "For her path sinks down to death, / and her footsteps lead to the shades." The author of the proverb wants to make a point, namely, that involvement with a seductress who is married can lead to grave social consequences beyond merely personal sin.

C. *Fable:* An imaginative tale in which the actors are animals or inanimate objects. They are made to say and do things in order to convey some moral lesson to humans. Proverbs 6:6–8 is an example of a fable: "Go to the ant, O sluggard, / study her ways and learn wisdom; / For though she has no chief, / no commander or ruler, / She procures her food in the summer, / stores up her provisions in the harvest." This proverb is a stinging indictment of the lazy person who acts as though no plans need to be made for the future. It is intended to rouse him from his torpor and make him take an active interest in planning out his life successfully.

D. *Irony:* A form of expression in which something other than what is actually said is meant for the sake of humor or sarcasm. "The sluggard loses his hand in the dish, / he will not even lift it to his mouth" (19:24). The sarcastic humor is intended to shake the lazy person out of his or her lethargy.

E. *Alliteration:* A literary device in which the same sound occurs at the beginning of words or of stressed syllables within words. Hebrew proverbs have many examples of alliteration, but most of these are lost in translation. But some renditions in English manage to preserve the alliteration without doing harm to the essential meaning: "The toiler's appetite toils for him" (16:26 AB).

F. *Pun:* A play on words with more than one meaning. Proverbs 23:27 says: "For the harlot is a deep ditch / and the adulteress a narrow pit." The "pit" may be Sheol, as in 7:27 and Psalm 30:4. But there may be a double meaning referring to the sexual role of the female. The Hebrew poets loved puns (see, e.g., Prov 22:14).[5]

G. *Personification:* A figure of speech in which things or abstract nouns are treated as if they were persons. For example, wisdom and folly are personified in 14:1.[6]

H. *Parable:* A story many of whose parts correspond to something in real life and that has a moral lesson attached to it. Proverbs 24:30–35 is an instance of a parable: "I passed by the field of the sluggard, / by the vineyard of the man without sense; / And behold! it was all overgrown with thistles; / its surface was covered with nettles, / and its stone wall broken down. / And as I gazed at it, I reflected; / I saw and learned the lesson: / A little sleep, a little slumber, / a little folding of the arms to rest.— / Then will poverty come upon you like a highwayman, / and want like an armed man." The picture of the untilled field is a sharply drawn cartoon of the lazy man.

Arrangement

The manner in which words or sentences are arranged, for the sake of effect, also plays a large part in the compiling of proverbs.

A. *Chiasm:* An arrangement in which the order of words in the first of two parallel clauses is reversed in the second. Proverbs 4:11–17 is a good illustration:

"Way of wisdom" (v. 11)—"Path of the wicked" (v. 14)

"Way of the wicked" (v. 19)—"Path of the just" (v .18)

If we write the clauses one below the other and draw diagonal lines to connect the words with similar meanings, the lines cross each other to form the Greek letter *chi*. Hence this arrangement is called a chiasm. It has an A-B-B-A structure.

B. *Acrostic:* The name given to Hebrew poetry in which each of the lines begins with a successive letter of the Hebrew alphabet.

Proverbs 2:1–22 and 31:10–31 are acrostic poems. This arrangement makes it easier to memorize the poem. There is a hidden symbolism in the acrostic that invites our consideration. It begins with the first alphabet *(aleph)*, ends with the letter *pe*, with the middle letter being *lamed*. Now, the middle letter comes from the root meaning "to teach." There is a subtle inference that Yahweh must guide the beginning, the middle, and the end of the teaching contained in the acrostic poem. That would give it the binding force of a divine oracle (2:5–6; 31:30).

C. *Inclusion:* A device for marking off a passage as a unit by placing it between two identical sentences with similar meaning. An instance of inclusion is the motto "The fear of the LORD." The sacred writer who performed the final editing of the book of Proverbs used this motto to mark off the first nine chapters as a unit (1:7 and 9:10). He also used it as an inclusion for the whole work (1:7 and 30:31).

D. *Parallelism:* In the classical tradition of Hebrew poetry, most of the proverbial sayings are arranged in parallel lines. The poetic art form consists in balancing one part of the proverb against the other part, in a regular three-beat-plus-three-beat meter. This kind of arrangement gives the proverb both solemnity and weight. For example:

> The glóry of-yoúng-men is-their-stréngth,
> And-the dígnity of-óld-men is-gráy-hair. (20:29)[7]

The *function* of such parallel arrangement is to serve as a mnemonic device for remembering and recalling the proverb.

Hidden in the proverbial saying is a cue-and-response mechanism that was widely used in the wisdom schools. Thus, in the two-line parallel form, the first line was intended to be spoken by the teacher, and the second line came as an antiphonal response from the pupils.

The *form* of the parallel takes on many variations.[8] Most of the proverbs come in two lines. Sometimes a third line is added (as in 19:7 AB), as an alternative to the second line. That such alternative forms of the same proverb were in circulation is seen by their appearance in different contexts (cf. 10:15 and 18:11, 11:13 and 20:19, 12:14 and 13:2). Occasionally we come across four-line wisdom sayings (as in 25:4–5, 6–7, 9–10). It is probable that the first pair is a cue and the second a response. The very presence of such variations shows that they were more than merely mechanical responses on the part of the pupil. A good teacher would be happy and proud to preserve the different responses of some of his brighter pupils that he thought were apt. It would be one way to reward the originality and creativity of his pupils.

Sometimes the teacher might even challenge the pupils to discover a parallel not expressly stated. We find a sample of this technique in 18:17: "The man who pleads his case first / seems to be in the right; / then his opponent comes and puts him to the test." By recasting the second line, "But under cross-examination he can be proved wrong," we discover a parallel that is antithetical to the first.

We see another example of a hidden parallel in 20:14: " 'Bad, bad!' says the buyer; / but once he has gone his way, he boasts." We can make explicit the parallel by rewording the saying thus:

"When a man is bargaining, he devalues his purchase, / but when he has bought it, he exaggerates its value."

Kinds of Parallelism

A. *Synonymous Parallelism:* The second line more or less says what the first line says. For instance: (1) "Evil men must bow down before the good, / and the wicked, at the gates of the just" (14:19). (2) "The ear that hears, the eye that sees — / The LORD has made them both" (20:12); put differently: "The Lord makes the ear to hear; / He also makes the eye to see."

Some proverbs of comparative degree are also types of synonymous parallelism: "Better a lowly man who supports himself / than one of assumed importance who lacks bread"(12:9).

B. *Antithetic Parallelism:* The second line says the opposite of what the first line says: "The memory of the just will be blessed, / but the name of the wicked will rot" (10:7).

C. *Synthetic Parallelism:* The second line is an elaboration or extension of the first. There are many variations of this type:

(1) The second line completes or develops the thought of the first line: "The sluggard loses his hand in the dish; / he will not even lift it to his mouth" (19:24).

(2) The second line provides an additional predicate to the subject mentioned in the first: "He who listens to salutary reproof / will abide among the wise" (15:31).

(3) The first line supplies the antecedent of a conditional statement; the second, the consequent: "When the LORD is

pleased with a man's ways, / he makes even his enemies be at peace with him" (16:7).

(4) The second line points out the result of what is said in the first line: "The bread of deceit is sweet to a man, / but afterward his mouth will be filled with gravel" (20:17).

(5) The second line gives the reason for what is said in the first: "Balance and scales belong to the LORD; / all the weights used with them are his concern" (16:11) The Anchor Bible offers this comment: "A set of stone weights of 1, 2, 4, and 8 shekels (= 2/ 5 oz avdp) were kept in a bag or pouch. With these four weights any number of shekels up to 15 could be weighed. Stoneweights of much larger multiples were also in use. One representing 8 minas or 400 shekels (=10 lbs) came from Tel Beit Mirsim."[9]

Another example is "Kings have a horror of wrongdoing, / for by righteousness the throne endures" (16:12).

Now You Can Enter the Writing Contest

The skill and ingenuity of proverb making demonstrates that the sages who authored them were superb craftsmen.[10] The mission of the ancient Egyptian and Babylonian wisdom schools was precisely this: to turn out "craftsmen of speech." They were to be masters of the word, equal to every occasion. Their training was to equip them to utter the seasonal word: the right word, at the right time, in the right place, to the right person, in the right measure.

Wisdom herself is personified as a "craftsman" who designs this universe according to an orderly plan. Wisdom's skill in ordering the whole of creation is equally at work ordering her human creation. Beginning with the king, the royal court, and the scribal profession, the habit and contagion of wisdom was to spread like leaven through the whole of society. Only then would moral order permeate society in imitation of the physical order that prevails in the universe.

There was an outburst of literary activity in the wisdom schools founded by King Solomon. There was a meeting of minds, a contest of wits, that continually helped prune and perfect the final product: the *mashal,* or proverb as we know it today. This constant engaging of minds forced teacher and pupil alike to think on their feet. It called for discipline, hard work, and study on their part. It is not utterly inconceivable that the eager pupils were given written exercises in which they were to come up with new proverbs or new applications of the old wisdom teaching to ever-changing situations. But above all they were to cultivate joy in workmanship. The costly effort of creative writing, thinking, and speaking might have been futile were it not also, and even more, a labor of love.

We too can feel this pulse of creative energy coursing through us as we are drawn to discover our own vocation as creative writers. If, in an average English class, we were to ask the students how many would like to become writers, their hands would likely go up ten to one. And yet, it is perhaps only one out of the ten who might succeed in achieving any distinction as a writer. As miniature essays or miniature stories, proverbs invite us to become writers, to write our own story, and to create our own essay. They also offer us the hope that, with a little sustained effort on our part, we will succeed.

What makes one a writer? To become a writer, we must have something to say and we must be able to say it effectively. We need ideas; we also need to clothe them with the proper expression so as to communicate them in an effective way. Proverbs contain both elements: they have a content; they also have a form. They offer us some piece of wisdom for every occasion. They also communicate that wisdom in a crisp, clear, attractive, and pleasing manner.

In an essay, "Milton and the Grand Style," John Galsworthy distinguished between two classes of writers. The first consists of those who have ready ideas at their disposal and encounter little difficulty finding the right expression with which to communicate them. Shakespeare belongs to this class. To the second belong those who have ready access to words; but they have to struggle, by dint of effort, until they come up with an idea. Milton belongs to this second class. A facsimile of a page in *Paradise Lost* shows that almost every line is gone over again and again until Milton is satisfied it expresses what he wants to say. To whichever of these classes we may belong, we can use proverbs as models for improving our writing skills. As an ancient Latin saying has it: *Fabricando fabri fimus* (By working we become workmen).

Where do we begin? The starting point of all writing is having something to say. The greater our familiarity with a subject, the better will we be equipped to write about it. Proverbs are the product of life experiences. So, the more intensely and profoundly we experience life, the better will we become empowered to capture those experiences in fitting language. By and large, experience provides the basis for most of the content of what we have to say. It matters little if the experience is our own or someone else's.

Once we have the subject matter in place (what we are going to write about), we then attend to the form (how to say it effectively). The heartbeat of a proverb is the comparison. Looking for similes in nature, finding the apt analogy, can help to make our sentences more striking and colorful instead of stilted and dull.

Furthermore, proverbs offer us a wide variety of techniques for making every word count. By attending to the form, we can learn to make our thoughts and expressions picturesque, pointed, witty, or sarcastic as the circumstance demands. Or by simply rearranging the words or creating the right balance, we can touch up our ideas so as to make them crisp and clear as well as pithy and profound.

Proverbs provide copious examples of how the sages achieved these effects. They are, after all, interpretations of what the sages observed in life. By comparing, contrasting, classifying, reflecting, and drawing conclusions, the masters teach us how we can make our thoughts more colorful, pleasing, forceful, convincing, and enduringly to be treasured. As keen observations and commentaries of human character and behavior, proverbs are proof that whatever is uniquely personal, or of interest to us, is likely to be felt as equally personal or of interest to others.

Writing need not be a drudgery, despite the costly effort it takes. Proverbs teach us that there can be joy in creativity and workmanship. Not only "A thing of beauty is a joy forever," as

Now Let's All Have a Little Fun!

Keats visioned, but the pursuit of writing with joy can help us to find beauty in the activity itself. *Paidia*, the Play Way in education, writing for fun, enjoying each step of the writing process will in the end leave its indelible mark on the finished product. What is true of the proverb is also true of the big story.

In the end, there is only one tested and tried principle for becoming a good writer. It is simply this: Write at least ten lines every day on something that you feel deeply and strongly about. In time you will become an accomplished writer.

Chapter 15

The Dynamics of a Numerical Saying

The numerical proverb has an art form of its own. In the three-four form, for instance, the climactic fourth line cumulatively sums up and surpasses the qualities of the objects described in the preceding three.

There is more to numbers than what meets the eye. The midrash on Proverbs 30:18–19 explains how.

Many centuries ago a wisdom teacher made this observation to a prince about to be married:

> Three things are too wonderful for me,
>   yes, four I cannot understand:
> The way of an eagle in the air,
>   the way of a serpent upon a rock,
> The way of a ship on the high seas,
>   and the way of a man with a maiden. (30:18–19)

What made the sage feel astonished? What was it he could not fathom?

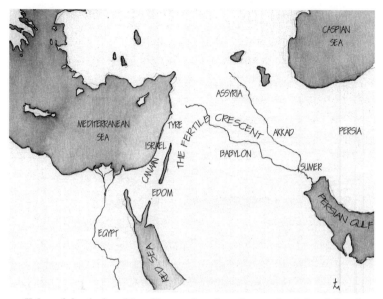

"Map of the Ancient Near East and nations famous for their wisdom."

Was the sage wondering how movement takes place without any visible trace of propulsion? Or perhaps was he marveling how human love bears a striking similarity to the three things observed in the external world? The eagle that soars, the serpent that glides, the ship that sails, though each mysterious in its own way, yet together they highlight the enduring power of human love. As the lover in King Solomon's famous Song of Songs says to his beloved: "Set me as a seal on your heart, / as a seal on your arm; / For stern as death is love, / Its flames are a blazing fire. / Deep waters cannot quench love, / nor floods sweep it away" (8:6).

This ancient numerical saying, couched in the form of a riddle, raises puzzling questions. What makes two persons in love commit themselves to a binding relationship for life? What gives them the courage to make such a radical decision in the face of life's uncertainties? How can they be sure that they will be faithful till death before life has even dealt out its hand?

The sage's wonderment seems to suggest that the riddle itself contains the answer: is not this, after all, the very nature of love? Sometimes the feeling of love can be so exhilarating that it takes off like a soaring eagle. Listen to our best love poems, and you will get the impression of the soul soaring toward the skies without the thought of never reaching there and without the fear of falling to the ground. Love's power enables us to glide over rough spots in life like the serpent across a rock. Sometimes love enables us to sail like a ship over troubled waters. As in each of the four instances, love manages to find ways to forge ahead despite the resistance of contrary forces. The sage's wonderment gives the prince and us much food for thought. Even the three-and-four form of the numerical saying, totaling up to the number seven, has important implications.

Now Let's Play the Game of Numbers

Numbers play an important part in Hebrew poetry. The number three stands for God, four for the earth, and seven for completion or perfection. The implication here is that when the wisdom of God guides our human wisdom, it makes a perfect combination. Also, the climactic fourth line contains and surpasses the qualities of the objects described in the preceding three. The original saying was probably part of an ancient Egyptian collection. Centuries later a scribe of the Hebrew school of wisdom copied down this numerical saying and made it a permanent part of a collection of Hebrew proverbs. In so doing, he gave the popular saying a new meaning by weaving it into a unique conception of *Yahweh,* the Hebrew word for God.

A Midrash on Proverbs 30:18–19

When God looked for an image to describe himself, he found it in marriage. The way in which God loves us is like that by which a husband loves his wife. Such a comparison may simplify somewhat our understanding of God, but it also deepens the mystery of human love. In the book of Genesis we are told that male and female are, together, not separately, the image and likeness of God (Gen 1:27). In marriage the union of a man and a woman brings into being a new creation, a new reflection of God. When God puts his love into our hearts, he imparts something of himself. God empowers us to do what human love promises but love alone cannot keep—namely, to be faithful to each other till death. In married love we get a glimpse of how God loves: not grudgingly but generously; not for a time only but always; not self-servingly but, if need be, even sacrificially.

Weddings last but a day; a marriage is for a lifetime. All the more reason therefore to seal our promise with a vow so as to guard ourselves against the fickleness of subsequent decision. Marriage is least of all about contracts and agreements; it is most of all about love. There are only two words in the vocabulary of love: *you* and *always. You* because love is *unique; always* because love is *enduring.*

In the language of human relationships, the pronoun *you* is sacred. It is the realm of infinite space as well as of infinite surprises. And when one is truly in love, the word *you* is spoken with utmost devotion. Martin Buber, the German-Jewish philosopher and mystic, explains that "in every I-YOU relationship the Eternal YOU shines forth."[1] That is why it takes three to get married: a man, a woman, and God. So great is the mystery of marriage.

Because marriage is a graced event, husband and wife can dare to love as God loves. Paul explains how in his inspired eulogy on love: "Love is patient; love is kind. Love is not jealous, it does not put on airs, it is not snobbish. Love is never rude, it is not self-seeking, it is not prone to anger; neither does it brood over injuries. Love does not rejoice in what is wrong but rejoices with the truth. There is no limit to love's forbearance, to its trust, its hope, its power to endure" (1 Cor 13:4–7). What a way to live! When man and wife love each other that way, they come close to reproducing the love that is divine.

The reading goes on to say that "love never fails" (4:8). Of the three things that endure—namely, faith, hope, and love—the greatest of these is love.

The riddle about human love, given by the ancient sage, finds its ultimate answer in the mystery of Christian marriage. God's Spirit descends upon the couple as they exchange their vows at God's holy altar. From there on, their journey is marked by unmistakable signs of God's presence. In moments when their love soars toward the heavens, God allows them to catch a glimpse of his goodness. Sometimes he empowers them to glide smoothly over rough spots so that no disappointment or setback may mar the harmony and sanctity of their married bliss. He lets their trust in each other carry them safely through the troubled waters of life if and when they come, as indeed they must, so that no suffering or sorrow or loss may deprive them of the riches of their inheritance.

In time their love bears fruit in children, a heavenly Father's precious gift to them, each a unique manifestation of his goodness. Then their love spills over into an ever-widening circle of friends, who in turn will be refreshed, energized, and transformed by the radiant warmth of their love. At times God even allows the breezes of heaven to blow through every space where they dwell, celebrate, entertain, discourse, or transact business. He blesses them in all their relationships and lets them glow with the warmth of his presence.

God gives them length of days so that they may enjoy the fruit of their labors. He brings them at last to that safe haven of rest where, through the corridors of time, beyond the pillars of death, they shall know at last that all their yesterdays and all their tomorrows were but echoes of the heartbeat of God's everlasting love. The riddle of the sage finds its answer in the mystery of divine love.

Chapter 16

"The Faithful Wife!" Is She for Real? Or Is She a Figment of the Imagination?

Proverbs 31:10–31, "The Faithful Wife," is at once an acrostic poem, an imitation of a marriage song, and a poem of wisdom in action. In this threefold art form, "The Faithful Wife" is a vindication of true womanhood as well as of wisdom itself.

By reason of its structure as well as its content, Proverbs 31:10–31 forms a fitting conclusion to the whole book. It says in a poetic and practical way what wisdom is all about.

This section of Proverbs is an acrostic poem on the good wife. It consists of twenty-two stanzas. Each begins with a successive letter of the Hebrew alphabet. The poem develops in greater detail the thought of Proverbs 18:22: "He who finds a wife finds happiness; / it is a favor he receives from the LORD." The stage has already been set for such a development by what has gone before. The theme of the good wife figures prominently in 11:16; 12:4; 18:22; and 19:14. There we find the acknowl-

"A clever woman is never without wool."

edgement that such a woman doesn't come by easily. She is a mark of divine favor. Not only does she earn her husband's trust; he in turn reaps rich rewards for his trust in terms of peace, prosperity, happiness, well-being, and a long life.

Some of the qualities of the good wife are what one might expect to find in an average household. She is diligent in caring for her family. She foresees their needs and makes ample provision for them. She makes every effort to see that they are well fed, well clothed, and well cared for.

She is portrayed as being thrifty and efficient in running the household. Under normal conditions this task would have been carried out by the husband. But his duties as a judge call upon him frequently to settle disputes at the city gate (31:23). Because of these lengthy absences away from home, she is obliged to take over the duties of managing the domestic affairs. She buys all the provisions in advance. She selects what is best, even if she has to go far to find it (31:14). She is economical: she buys the raw materials out of which she manufactures and designs her own clothing for herself and the family (31:13, 17, 19, 25). She is industrious. In order to discharge her duties efficiently, she rises very early in the morning and works till late at night (31:15–16). What keeps her so busy? How does she manage her time?

As we take a closer look, we discover that she is more than a good wife; she is the perfect wife. She is one of a kind (31:10). There is none like her (31:29). Verses 10 and 29 form an inclusion. The poem is written in the wisdom tradition of a marriage song, similar to the one we find in Song of Songs 7:1–10. It is a song in praise of a bride. In the traditional marriage song, the bride's beauty is the subject of praise. But in Proverbs the emphasis is more on her business acumen and managerial skills. The poet's meticulous attention to detail gives the poem a sense of completion. The author of the poem doesn't want to leave anything out. She is applauded for making wise investments in real estate With the profits she makes, she expands her substantial holdings (31:16). An Arab proverb states: "A clever woman is never without wool."[1] Unlike the fool or the lazy person, this ideal wife is always prepared. With the skill of her own hands, she manufactures products for the use of her family, including even the household furnishings (31:22). She successfully markets the surplus of goods she has made, including garments and scarves, and makes lucrative sales with them (31:22, 24, 25). No wonder she is honored as a woman of high standing within the community. Her praises are sung far and wide (31:28–31). The poet describes her as if she were a finished product, almost picture perfect.

At a deeper level this worthy wife and mother is portrayed as the living symbol of wisdom herself.[2] She is *wisdom in action.* Proverbs 31:10–31 turns out to be an allegorical poem on wisdom. Many of the qualities ascribed to the faithful wife are descriptions of wisdom. She is the model of self-control, prudence, understanding, and just behavior. It is as though Lady Wisdom herself comes down from the exalted position she holds in Proverbs 1–9 and manifests herself in practical ways in the person of the worthy wife.

There are other subtleties that draw our attention to the close resemblance between the worthy wife and wisdom. Preparing sumptuous meals, making clothes, and engaging in commerce are metaphors for practical wisdom.

The mother sees to it that there is plenty of food for the body as well as for the mind (31:15, 26). The wine of wisdom and the bread of instruction are never in short supply, just as it always is at Lady Wisdom's banqueting table. Her kindness and mercy flow beyond the confines of the home. She gives out of her abundance to feed and clothe the poor and the unfortunate (31:20).

Her expertise in making and designing clothes also points to a close affinity to Lady Wisdom. Clothes well designed display elegantly the body's shape. They protect the body against the inclemencies of the weather. They accentuate the beauty of the personality. In the same way, wisdom forms, guards, and enriches the mind and spirit.

Her cleverness in handling commercial dealings is another sign of her kinship with Lady Wisdom. From ancient times Israel has engaged in making international exchanges of wisdom sayings with her Near Eastern neighbors. Many of these sayings crossed borders from one country to another: from Sumeria to Assyria, to Babylon, to Egypt, to Israel. These exchanges took place frequently and freely, resulting in many different collections. They were seen as commercial transactions. While Israel has its own collection, she borrows from other cultures what is best and what can easily be integrated into her own religious tradition. "The fear of the LORD" was the guiding principle for integrating the wisdom of other cultures, just as it was the guiding principle of the worthy wife's virtuous life and of her successful commercial enterprises (31:30). The search would lead to faraway places. Because she has done so well for herself, her praises are sung by all, even at the city gate.

Proverbs 31:10–31 is a work of highly artistic creation. In the person of the worthy wife, the poet sings the praises of Lady Wisdom. One is the echo of the other. By using the art forms of an allegory, a marriage song, and an acrostic, the poet wants to show that both are unique creations. Wisdom, as "the first of God's creation," is one of a kind. She cannot be duplicated, as Dame Folly unsuccessfully tries to do. Nor is there any ploy for unseating her. What is true of wisdom is also true of her protégés, one of whom is the faithful wife. They will endure as long as wisdom abides in them. Wisdom first built her house on a hill, supported by seven pillars. Now she has found herself a second home. She finally settles down in her new house to serve those who have accepted her invitation. Thus the portrait of the good wife serves as an interpretative framework for the whole book.

Is She for Real? Or Is She a Figment of the Imagination?

So the question arises whether such a woman really exists. It is reasonable to believe that the author knew a definite woman who fitted this description. Most of the duties she performed were those that most women normally carried out, such as rising early and working till late at night, providing for the family.

But this particular woman also happens to be a member of an elite class. She wields a great deal of power and influence. Proverbs 31:21–23 makes allusions to wealth and nobility: "fine linen and purple are her clothing" (31:22) might suggest that she has royal connections. Her husband is also an upstanding member of the upper class. He is a judge of some sort who sits with the elders to settle disputes at the city gate. While he is away on business, his wife runs a tight schedule, giving detailed instructions to her maid servants. The Anchor Bible translation has an additional line in verse 13 that suggests the idea. The woman is also highly skilled and self-reliant, independently wealthy but not wasteful. With her own hands she turns out lovely linens, bed coverings, articles of clothing, garments, belts, scarves, and other household furnishings. With these she provides for her family as well as runs a profitable business. Even though this is not the average woman we come across in Near Eastern societies, we know that such women did exist. The queen of Sheba is one such example. But such women were the exception. The Anchor Bible translation is up-front in admitting, "She is a rare find" (31:10). In any case, she is not a figment of the imagination. Much less is she a cinderella princess waiting to be rescued by her knight in shining armor.

The author of the poem has exploited the noble qualities of the faithful wife to paint a portrait of Lady Wisdom. Many of the nuances in the descriptions are common to both. Their worth is more precious than jewels. They are women of "many parts." They have a noble origin. They show extreme foresight and thoughtfulness in providing for the needs of those under their care.[3] They lavish largesses out of their abundance to care for the less fortunate. They seek out only what is best in order to bring peace, contentment, security, happiness, well-being, health, and longevity. Those invited to the table can be sure that there is more than enough for all. They are women of stature and virtue. They are models of diligence and never encourage laziness in those under their care. What they have to offer is always good, never what is harmful. They work tirelessly night and day. No wonder their praises are sung by all. They are esteemed before God and men. Their house is a place of refuge for all who live in it. Hospitality abounds. There is no lack of food or clothing to nurture and protect bodies, nor of wisdom to enhance the mind. Their ultimate secret of living wisely lies in their common reverence for the Lord. Wisdom has left her mark on the faithful wife to the extent that the latter has become a living example of practical wisdom.

Conclusion

Is Proverbs All About Women:
Their Rise to Fame? Their Fall to Shame?
Where Are All the Wise Men Gone?

Proverbs begins as a training school for young men. Their training consists in the princely art of wisdom. It is meant primarily for future kings, their sons and daughters, their counselors, the officials of the royal court, and the members of the scribal profession. Proverbs ends with a poetic profile of the faithful wife, who is a living exhibit of wisdom itself.

Sandwiched between these two, the trainees and the faithful wife, are at least five graphic descriptions of fallen women. The trainees are put on guard against the lewd, the lecherous, the loose woman. She is described as "a stranger woman."[4] She is a foreigner who does not share their mores. The young men are reminded of their own vulnerability to the seductive charms of such a woman. She would think nothing at all about luring them into a trap by exposing them to her seductive wiles. A single exposure could result in their undoing. They would lose their innocence as well as the wisdom they have worked so long and hard to obtain. In Proverbs, sexual indulgence seems to be the pivotal sin that paves the way for every other license to do whatever one pleases even if it is wrong, evil, or harmful. For this reason Proverbs comes down hard on the temptress with the harshest condemnation. She is described again and again as a harlot, a "deep ditch" (23:27), with the smell of death in her belly. She leads the way to Sheol, from which there is no return. At the same time, Proverbs assumes that the good wife is hard to find. When found, she is to be regarded as a blessing from God. She is like a fresh spring in a garden of delights, bringing refreshment to her husband.

Proverbs is an unfolding drama whose two main characters are Lady Wisdom and Dame Folly. The rest of us are their prospective clients. To the undiscerning eye, they seem very much alike. They resemble each other in many ways. They both have built their houses on a hill, which gives them a vantage point to survey the terrain below. They both go out in search of clients. They both send out invitations to a banquet where only the best viands are provided. They both have an array of servants to help them in the preparations and in their services to their guests. They both make their pitch to the simple hearted.

And yet, despite their similarities, they are poles apart. Dame Folly, as it turns out, is ultimately recognized as a caricature of Lady Wisdom; but not by all. Lady Wisdom exalts and uplifts, while Dame Folly dismantles and destroys. One brings only good and never any harm; the other brings evil in her train. One leads to the "tree of life" (3:18), the other to death and destruction.

Is Proverbs, then, all about women: their rise to fame, their fall to shame? To be sure, the wisdom teachers who administer the curriculum are mostly males. But hovering around the hallways of the wisdom schools is the animating presence and spirit of Lady Wisdom. She is constantly by our side in order to exorcise the fool that lurks within each of us. But within us is also the capacity for discerning and receiving wisdom. It is our God-given endowment. She will exploit this capacity to the fullest by whetting our appetite to search for her until we have found her. She would like to make herself our permanent possession before Dame Folly can even have a chance to lay her traps. She offers us the hope that wisdom is possible to attain. But it requires hard work, constant study, and moral discipline. It is nurtured within the protective environment of both home and school and the constant company of the wise. It would seem that the makers and wreckers of wisdom are both women who inspire their followers to scale the heights of wisdom or slide down the slippery slopes of folly. So we may ask: Where are all the wise men gone?

Proverbs' answer to this question seems to be that only a few succeed in making wisdom their life's vocation. Among these are likely to be the king when he is graced to act as God's oracle. The counselor, the scribe, the wisdom teacher who have heeded wisdom's call and, by dint of effort and study, have learned to make wisdom a habit could also be counted among wisdom's success stories. But above all, wisdom comes to abide in the parent who heeds her instruction and passes it on to his or her children. The final redemption against all the evil that men and women in society have wrought is the faithful wife. Wisdom may have been proferred as a princely art. But it requires the queenly virtues of docile obedience and fidelity to her teaching and ultimately "reverence for the LORD." This is Proverbs' way of vindicating the honorable role that women are called upon to play.

Chapter 17

The Magisterial Role of Proverbs

Their Solomonic ring,
Their noble lineage,
Their ancient pedigree,
The sublimity of their message,
Their nourishment from the source,
The awesome authority that they exercise,
Their timeliness, relevance, and evenhandedness,
Their ecumenical quality, and
The enduring place they have found in the
Scriptures—All conspire to give proverbs a
magisterial role to play.

Within the field of wisdom literature, proverbs play a magisterial role. This is largely due to their attribution to King Solomon and to his reputation for having surpassed the wisdom of the people of the East and all the wisdom of Egypt. Proverbs offer the kingly art of wisdom to a kingly people. But they also demand the queenly art of receptivity for the wisdom to become appropriated. Proverbs have the capacity to pick up the most common among us and make us worthy to dine with kings at their banqueting table.

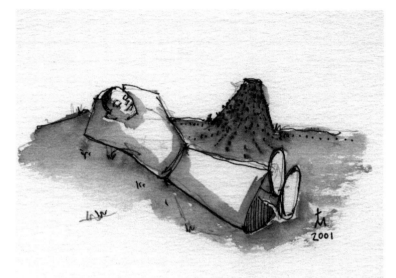

Proverbs 6:6 *"Go to the ant, O Sluggard, study her ways and learn wisdom..."*

Proverbs spring from a noble lineage. Many of the so-called proverbs of Solomon were composed in the scribal academies of ancient Sumer. They came into full blossom during the Sumerian renaissance between 1700 and 1200 B.C.E. Others were compiled in the royal courts of Egypt. The standard formula for introducing the instruction genre, which is an Egyptian import, was "Hear, my son, your father's instruction, / and reject not your mother's teaching" (Prov 1:8).[1] This introductory formula recurs in every division of Proverbs (cf. 1:8; 10:1; 22:17; 29:3; 31:1–9).

Others had a more humble origin. Similar appeals to a parent's teaching were made in order to pass on the ancient wisdom of Israel's tribal past: "Listen to your father who begot you, / and despise not your mother when she is old" (23:22). This saying deals with the family as the source of wisdom, which is sometimes referred to as clan wisdom. Many of Israel's proverbs were borrowed from her immediate neighbors. Among these, Phoenician Tyre and Edom were both renowned for their wisdom. Proverbs 8–9 is full of Canaanite words and expressions and may go back to Phoenician sources more directly than any other material in that book. Here and there we find examples of "royal" wisdom, for example, in 8:14–16; 28:16; and 29:4, 14. Many of the other proverbs found their way into Israel all the way from Arabia, traveling along the caravan routes or possibly by way of the Diaspora Jews who, since the eighth century B.C.E., had become permanently settled along the Fertile Crescent. It is also conceivable that the exiles returning from captivity had brought with them their own repertoire of collections of proverbs from Babylon, Assyria, and even distant Persia.

Notwithstanding their humble origins, these proverbs bear the marks of a finished product. They had been worked over and refined by scribal professionals into a literary work of art. In this fashion, proverbs came to possess an aristocracy of their own. Like thoroughbreds primed for the race, they had been made ready for use in the scribal schools. They exhibit their royal connections by the sheer nobility of their expression and the simple, upright, and honest manner in which they make their frequent invitations to virtuous living.

Quite apart from their noble lineage, proverbs also have an ancient and revered pedigree. Most of the proverbs attributed to King Solomon go back way beyond Solomon himself. Proverbs traveled far and wide before they became parts of collections. In every region through which they passed, they discovered a family of connections: a brother, a sister, or a distant cousin. Soon there arose collections around the same theme. The tree line of family relationships spread across regional and cultural boundaries Newer and newer collections were found in different regions, saying almost the same thing in similar or different words. From out of this rich and inexhaustible source of collections, many of the wisdom sayings were trimmed, pruned, and carefully transplanted into Israel's religious tradition until they found at last an enduring place in what has come to be known in the Hebrew Bible as the book of Proverbs.

Perhaps what is most Solomonic about the so-called proverbs of Solomon are the 375 sayings arranged in mostly two-line poetic parallel form between Proverbs 10:1 and 22:16.[2] Both the number 375 and the poetic form are artificial contrivances designed to give the proverbs, many of which were cultural imports, a more Solomonic ring. This middle section is also presumed by scholars to be the oldest of the collections. Within this segment there may well be a few proverbs that go back to Israel's golden age, such as 14:28–35; 16:10–15; 20:2, 8, 26, 28; 25:1–7. After all, it was in court circles, and especially in the wisdom schools that King Solomon founded, that the wisdom movement in Israel began to flourish. Even though Solomon may not have authored many of the proverbs attributed to him, still his presence and the spirit of wisdom associated with his name animates them. Because of him they have come to be revered till this day as wisdom sayings.

Another reason proverbs play a magisterial role is that the wisdom they contain receives its constant nourishment from the source, God. The very attempt to integrate secular wisdom into the Hebrew religious tradition makes this connection obvious. In one way or another, all the proverbs point to God as the ultimate source of human wisdom and the goal of every human search for it.

This is made more explicit by the motto that runs through the entire work and is stated at the beginning in 1:7. From this insertion of the motto at the beginning, the middle, and the end, we can draw but one conclusion that the author would like us to keep in mind. It is simply this: the subterranean streams that must constantly nourish and feed proverbial wisdom and steer it away from going astray come from one ever present and unfailing source: the fear of the Lord, which is the beginning of wisdom. If the compass of the heart were not habitually directed to promoting piety, then the wisdom that guides human conduct would sooner or later lose its binding force.

The insertion of the wisdom poem (Proverbs 8) and the parable of the two banquets (Proverbs 9) into the middle of the book further strengthens this thesis: human wisdom must find its ultimate guidance in divine wisdom. Wisdom's self-eulogy touches the sublime in 8:22–31 She stakes out the claim that wisdom's origin comes ultimately not from men but from God. With the measured ease of a consummate craftsman, she brings into being a well-ordered universe, just as she works to bring an orderly existence into our lives. Wisdom's exalted position empowers her to give bounteously out of her inexhaustible treasury. She prepares a royal banquet with the best vintage wine of wisdom and the fresh, nourishing bread of instruction. And yet, despite her generosity, she exemplifies the greatest economy. She gives without any waste and without any dissipation of her gifts.

Despite their noble lineage and their ancient pedigree, proverbs make their pitch to the simple hearted with a certain awesome authority. "So now" is how wisdom closes her exhortation in 8:32. With subtlety, but also without dishonesty, she makes her appeal: in choosing her, to choose life; and in rejecting her, to consign ourselves forever to become lovers of death (8:36). Key words in this closing exhortation are *listen, obey, watch, wait, find,* and *win* (8:34–35). These words outline the receptive mode for appropriating the wisdom offered to us. With a tone of finality, the choice that proverbs offer us is ultimately the choice between life and death. How awesome to know that wisdom is within easy reach of those determined to find her! How frightening to realize that, in straying away from the source, we covet death! The simple who seek her and find her are to be distinguished from those "who lack understanding" (9:4). How refreshing to know that simplicity need be no barrier to the acquisition of wisdom! The open-mindedness with which even the simple-hearted can attain wisdom fit for kings gives point to the adage that even "a cat can look at a king."[3] The very activity of gaining wisdom is itself a mark of intelligence.

In Proverbs, two clear models of simplicity where wisdom finds a home are the trusting child and the faithful wife. Proverbs emphasizes the fact that the child who is obedient and carries out faithfully what the parents have taught will go far in leading a happy, secure, and successful life. Proverbs also eulogizes conjugal fidelity as a divinely ordained institution and celebrates the faithful wife as a spring in a garden of delights. Proverbs lacks words to describe her hidden beauty, just as it does regarding wisdom. The hind and the doe are for the oriental poet symbols of grace and feminine beauty.[4] Wisdom gravitates to wherever simplicity is to be found: in the child, whose heart has been prepared through long years of training in docility and obedience to appropriate the wisdom learned over the years; in the faithful wife, because the fear of the Lord has guided her steadily all through life, making her a fit receptacle for wisdom to find a dwelling place. It is to such as these that wisdom makes her appeal. They are the simple hearted: those with open minds to listen to what she has to say and docilely to follow her counsels.

Another contributing reason for the status that proverbs enjoy is that, by reason of their antiquity, they come well tried and tested. They resonate to our common everyday experiences. They are constant reminders of all the foolish vanities with which we frequently indulge ourselves. They so accurately describe the error of our ways. And when we are fortunate enough to surpass ourselves by reaching a high degree of nobility of conduct, we measure our success by the standards they have set. Wherever we go, whichever way we turn, proverbs confront us as our mentors, our teachers, our guides, and sometimes even as our critics and judges. There is no recourse against their counsels and no escape from their admonitions and warnings. We live by their light and fall by the choices we ourselves have made.

Even though their application is in space and time, proverbs are beyond space and time. Proverbs have been with us since time began. Their origins are lost in history. They have crossed time, space, and cultural barriers from Sumer to Babylon, to Assyria and Egypt. They have come from Persia and Arabia to Tyre, to Edom, to Canaan to find at last a permanent resting place in Israel. From wherever they may have originated, they have found a way into almost every home. Wherever wisdom is cherished, proverbs have managed to win a hearing. Wherever humans have had keen insights or have intensely experienced life, proverbs have emerged as handy devices for framing those insights and enshrining those experiences. Though beyond space, they make their ubiquitous presence felt everywhere. Though timeless, their relevance to every situation has been keenly sensed. Everywhere that humans gather for discourse, proverbs attest to the presence of wisdom, our need for it, and the equally present danger of folly laying traps to lure us away from wisdom.

In every age proverbs have demonstrated their usefulness as ready substitutes for lengthy discourses. They have done so with effect, one might add. They have been treasured as wisdom sayings clothed in clever art forms. They have come to be loved and appreciated for their brevity packed with punch. They give us something to say, something to do, something to hope for, also something to avoid or run away from.

Their stated purpose is to live rightly (1:3). To this end, they offer to the understanding wholesome teaching about true wisdom, and to the will powerful incentives for the right ordering of our lives. The counsels of proverbs embrace all human activity and are calculated to cultivate in us a certain measure of practical sagacity, sound judgment, and resourcefulness for the successful management of our lives. With simplicity and moral discipline in place, proverbs teach us how to cultivate nobility of speech that will make us pleasing to God and win the esteem of our fellow human beings in society.

As we begin to mature, we come to realize the transcendent nature of wisdom. It may have taken shape within us, but proverbs remind us that it was there before us. We may have framed the discourse, but we are always its servitors. Wisdom is the breath of God animating his creation (20:27). We only breathe by that divine breath whenever we utter the discourse that contains wisdom. When we meet persons who are truly wise, it is not so much that they possess wisdom; it is rather that wisdom possesses them. We often take credit for what is not wholly ours, like the rich man who boastingly pointed to his garden and said: "My garden!" The gardener smiled.

Proverbs are no respectors of persons. They direct their counsels and administer their warnings without partiality to princes and people alike. They speak with equal authority to the great and the small, the rich and the poor, the weak and the strong, the high and the lowly, without overly trying to please the one and without being overbearing toward the other. With evenhanded justice they bring down the mighty, scoff at the arrogant, exalt the lowly, laugh the fool to scorn, mock at the lazy, humor the hotheaded, and defend the poor and the oppressed. To those who feel secure in their possessions, proverbs warn against the emptiness of riches. To those suffering from want, they show that the poor need not be without their blessings. They warn against the pitfalls of passion, the uncertainty of riches, the danger of ill-gotten gain, the lure of quick sexual gratification. They are quick to snuff out the spark that flies from the contentious spirit before it can ignite the fires of strife and violence. They summon to justice the hidden intentions of the heart. They unmask the false pretensions that lie hidden beneath the human sagacity that naively parades as wisdom. They will search out every miscreant in society and expose "the man of Belial," the mischief maker, the man of lying speech (6:12–15). As a Spanish proverb says: "A lie has short legs. It can run, but in the end it will be caught."

Truth and justice are the two pivotal virtues around which most of the proverbs seem to gravitate. Truth, because it guarantees the inner integrity of the whole person before God and men. Justice, because it governs order in our relationships and brings about a balance in society between the fortunate and the unfortunate.

Above all, proverbs aim their deadliest darts at the wanton woman and reserve their sublimest praises for the faithful wife. The one, because she represents all that is evil, worthless, wicked, and vile; the other, because she stands for all that is good, noble, beautiful, and just. The one, because she stands forever poised to wreck the sanctity of marriage; the other, because she symbolizes wisdom steeped in the fear of the Lord and because she enjoys honor before God and men. The one is the supreme embodiment of folly as the other is the sublime manifestation of wisdom. In this struggle between wisdom and folly, the *quedesha,* the temple harlot, is revealed for who she really is. Together they are the ultimate paradigms of all that is worst and best in our humanity.

Proverbs make good conversation pieces. When they are humorously cited to illumine someone else's situation, we have the uneasy feeling that the other is really one of us. The other includes me. Even when the other is being lightheartedly held up for ridicule, there is a sense deep inside us that we too are being summoned to judgment. When we use a proverb to make others the butt of our jokes, we are at the same time laughing at ourselves. Proverbs often creep into our conversation, making us deeply aware of ourselves, of all that is true, good, and noble as well as of all that is silly, worthless, and evil.

Proverbs seem to have a life of their own. It is as though they are fully grown persons, self-contained, independent but never indifferent. They come and go as they please without our even noticing them. Sometimes we feel their palpitating presence in our midst. They fully engage us in all we do, think, and feel. We cannot avoid them, although we can refuse to let them have a say in our lives at our own peril. They can be our best friends or our worst enemies. They stand ready to serve as our trusted counsellors, or, if necessary, as our accusers in court. They can tease, taunt, goad, mock, and revile. They can also uplift, guide, and inspire. They can detect hidden motives, passions, feelings that surface from deep within and that, if allowed to go unchecked, could spell disaster. They teach us how to be esteemed when we are silent and how to gain a hearing when we speak. Proverbs are reality checks on our authenticity and on our openness to see the truth of things. Bit by bit they peel off the layers of fanciful conceits that surround our personality and cut us down to size.

Proverbs are ecumenical. They bring together and unite nations, peoples, and cultures, reminding us of our common experiences and also our common heritage. They make us participants in the common pool of wisdom that unites us all because it stems from our common humanity. The wisdom that proverbs offer is cohesive. It draws us closer to one another and to the fountainhead that is the common source of our life's nourishment: the wisdom that descends from above.

Proverbs play a vitally important leadership role in society, just as they did in the age of the prophets in Israel. In the centuries between 800 and 600 B.C.E., when the prophets surrounding the king gave political counsel, they often blurred the distinction between secular and spiritual wisdom. The enemies of Jeremiah acknowledged that the killing of prophets would not mean the disappearance of wisdom. Proverbs ensure that wisdom is here to stay and that when human guidance fails, there is always divine wisdom to guide us. We are never without recourse As long as we are humble enough to seek wisdom and are motivated by the fear of the Lord, wisdom will prevail. Such is the enduring hope that Proverbs holds out to us.

Even today, the secular wisdom that Proverbs offers is, for the most part, good. The divine wisdom it asks us to seek is better. In the last analysis, there need be no conflict between the two because, in the wisdom poem inserted in the middle of the work (8:1–36), wisdom is portrayed as the link between God and humans. Proverbs show how good men and women can find satisfaction and fulfillment in life, within a moral order, despite the perversity of evil persons. They show us how to steer our course successfully between human freedom and divine sovereignty. They lay down the principles for making the kinds of moral choices that will ensure justice, peace, and security and at the same time avert suffering and injustice in this world.

Above all, proverbs have won an enduring place in the scriptures. They operate alongside the ministry of the priest and the prophet as a kind of "third force." Even though the proverbs deal for the most part with purely secular wisdom, they nevertheless supplement the ministry of the priest and the prophet. And when any of those two branches of ministry fail, proverbs help them to get back on course by pointing to the higher wisdom that comes from God. It is truly astounding that some of the ancient civilizations that gave us many of their proverbs will one day share the blessings of true believers promised in Psalm 87:4. Inspired though not divinely revealed, proverbs are "useful for teaching—for reproof, correction, and training in holiness so that the man of God may be fully competent and equipped for every good work" (2 Tim 3:16–17).

Proverbs are golden nuggets of wisdom strewn in our way to guide us to our destiny. They teach us how to become esteemed among the living, to secure lasting immortality among the dead, and to rise as shining stars in the vaults of heaven. Such is the awesome majesty and grandeur of proverbial wisdom. The wisdom they offer is ours for the taking.

Notes

Chapter 1

1. Quoted in AB 3.

2. Quoted in *Learn Watercolor the Edgar Whitney Way,* by Ron Ranson, North Light Books, 1994, p. 12.

3. See TOL 21: "Proverbs are open-ended. They contain several layers of meaning."

4. See TOL 11: Proverbs are generalizations. Experience must provide the context in order to realize the point being driven; e.g, "The north wind usually brings rain (25:23). The fire of the kiln will doubtless purify precious metals (27:21). In the sphere of human conduct there is a correspondingly specific result to backbiting or to the effect of praise upon an individual."

5. Quoted in AB 3.

6. See CBC 5.

Chapter 2

1. See ANET 421–424. The connection between Proverbs and Amen-em-ope is fully discussed in CBC 76–85. See also AB 20.

2. Recent biblical scholarship provides ample evidence to show that similar writings ascribed to an author were really compiled by a later unknown editor who "cut up and combined the

source documents into a single story" (See WWB 23). A careful reading of the first nine chapters of Proverbs provides many hints that a later editor tried to give some kind of structure and unity to a series of unrelated and independent collections that had existed previously (see AB 20).

3. In WWB 39, Friedman makes the case that "the lengthy text known as the Court History of David (in the book of 2 Samuel) is a work which is both beautifully written and a remarkable example of history-writing, remarkable because it openly criticizes its heroes, a practice that is all but unknown among ancient Near Eastern kings."

See also AB, General Introduction, xxxi.

4. According to Friedman, in WWB 86, the two sources that contain the Joseph story (the E and the J) were written just about the time when Solomon became king. The J document was compiled between 846 and 722 B.C.E. and the E document between 922 and 722 B.C.E.

Chapter 3

1. See CCHS 500.

2. See DPW 191.

3. Proverbs 1:1–7 is "an introduction to *Proverbs* probably added by the final collector" (CCHS 500).

Chapter 4

1. A more profound reason for such a limitation is that wisdom ultimately partakes of the mystery of God. There are many proverbs that elucidate this point (See Prov 16:9, 20:24,

21:30–31). God alone knows how things will eventually turn out. Hence the foolishness of trusting entirely in our own resources for attaining wisdom (Prov 26:12).

2. See Carole Fontaine in "Proverbs," HBC 503.

Chapter 5

1. The first three strophes of Prov 2:1–22 (vv. 1–4, 5–8, 9–11) begin with the first letter of the Hebrew alphabet, *aleph*. The next three strophes (vv. 12–15, 16–19, 20–22) all begin with *lamed*, the middle letter of the Hebrew alphabet. They stress how wisdom "saves" (vv. 12, 16) those who follow her.

See also TOL 16 and 17. Roland Murphy makes this comment: "Even though wisdom is something to be pursued by common individual effort, it is essentially a gift of God (2:6)—one of the many paradoxes of the book."

2. Taken from the poem "I Grieved for Bonaparte," CPWW 177.

Chapter 6

1. Commenting on this motto, Roland Murphy has this to say: "The positioning of this verse…is important. It is the seventh verse, following upon the introduction, and it is repeated in 9:10, at the end of the first collection. Fear of the Lord also appears in 31:30, as a kind of inclusion to the book.…It is surely remarkable that a commitment to God lies at the basis of the wisdom enterprise" (TOL 16).

Chapter 7

1. This was first proposed by G. Bostrom, *Proverbiastudien: Die Weisheit und das Fremde Weib in Sir 1–9*, Lunds Universitets Arsskrift, n. f. A 1, vol. 30:3, Gleerup, 1935, cited in TOL 30, footnote 8.

Chapter 8

1. The phrase was coined by Francis Thompson in his immortal epic, "The Hound of Heaven." See CPFT 62.

2. The simple, straightforward, and honest speech of Lady Wisdom, disguised as a woman (8:6–7), is in sharp contrast to the smooth words and lying tongue of Dame Folly, who comes in the guise of an adulteress (6:24; 7:5).

3. Cf. Angelus Silesius, *The Cherub Pilgrim*, I, 68: "The abyss of my spirit calls forever with a cry to the abyss of God: Tell me which is deeper." Quoted in *The Discovery of God*, by Henri de Lubac, P.J. Kenedy and Sons, 1960, p. 13.

Chapter 9

1. Quoted by Josef Pieper in the front of his book *Happiness and Contemplation*, translated by Richard and Clara Winston, Pantheon Books, 1958.

Chapter 10

1. See CBC 39.

2. See TOL 137: "The remarkable speech of Lady Wisdom seems to have a very deliberate purpose within the book; if

Proverbs 1–9 is the 'introduction' to the collections of individual sayings that follow, this powerful motivating figure sweeps all the practical wisdom of Israel into the orbit of her activity."

3. No one builds a house without wisdom (Prov 24:3–4). And yet, the parody of Dame Folly trying to emulate Lady Wisdom is being sustained. Just as Lady Wisdom prefigures the "faithful wife" in Prov 31:10–33, so also Dame Folly becomes incarnate in the wiles of the "stranger" woman in Prov 2:18 and Proverbs 5–7.

Chapter 11

1. A proverb is said to be neutral when it is looked at from a purely practical point of view, without regard to ethical or moral considerations. In this context, *good* means whatever the world regards as the result of cleverness, or what gives us a decided advantage, or simply what appears to enhance life. By contrast, *bad* is what results from foolishness, or puts us at a disadvantage, or reduces the quality of life.

2. See Luke 16:19–31.

3. For a discussion on the origins of the different collections of proverbs, see *CBC* 51.

4. See notes on 10:1–7 in CBC 52.

Chapter 12

1. Ptah-hotep was the vizier of King Izezi of the Fifth Dynasty (about 2400 B.C.E.). See ANET 412.

2. Merikare, king of Upper and Lower Egypt, admonishes his son: "Be a craftsman of speech (so that) thou mayest be strong, (for) the tongue is a sword to (a man), and speech is more valorous

than fighting. No one can circumvent the skillful of heart.…They who know his wisdom do not attack him and no (misfortune) occurs where he is. Truth comes to him (fully) brewed, in accordance with the sayings of the ancestors" (ANET, 414–415).

3. See ANET 421. The Liturgical Press translation in CBC 76–77 is more modern and readable.

4. This commentary is taken from TOL 22.

5. See TOL, 8.

6. See ibid.

7. See CBC 61 (see also Prov 22:24).

8. See CBC 56.

9. See ibid.

10. See CBC 61.

11. See TOL 21.

12. See *Elements of Style,* 66.

13. A quotation from Francis Thompson's poem "The Kingdom of God" (see CPFT 357).

Chapter 13

1. See UOT 283.

2. CBC 78–85 shows the similarities between Proverbs and *The Instruction of Amenemope.* See also ANET 421–425.

3. See ANET 421–422.

4. See ANET 422.

5. See ANET 427–430.

Chapter 14

1. The Anchor Bible commentary suggests that the persistent use of parallelism "supports the assumption that the first line

was intended to be spoken by the teacher, calling forth the second line as an antiphonal response from the pupils" (see AB 18).

2. This is especially evident in the sudden appearance of a third and sometimes even a fourth line. The third line is inserted as an alternative to the second line (as in Prov 19:7). In a four-line parallel structure, the first pair is a cue and the second pair the response (see AB 18).

3. Many of the formulations in the succeeding pages are based on material contained in AB, 5–9.

4. See CCHS, comment on Prov 20:6.

5. Hebrew writers were skilled in making a play on words, sounds, and juxtapositions of participial phrases, as in 15:32. Most of these are lost in translation. See Murphy's comments under *Paranomasia* in TOL 6 and 7.

6. Wine is personified in Proverbs 20:1 as a proud and riotous person. In Proverbs 23:31 wine has "eyes." See comment on Proverbs 23:31 in TOL 133.

7. See CBC 25.

8. For a more extended discussion of forms, see Murphy in TOL 9–13.

9. See AB 106, footnote 11.

10. Murphy comments: "The sages had a flair for literary art. When they wrote about 'pleasing speech' (Pr. 16:21), and 'pleasant words' (16:24), they had in mind an aesthetic of words, not a content that would suit the pleasure of all" (see TOL 6).

Chapter 15

1. *I and Thou,* by Martin Buber, 2d ed., Charles Scribner's Sons, 1958, p. 6.

Chapter 16

1. Quoted in CBC 100.

2. The "finding" of a good wife is viewed as a great gift (Prov 18:22). So too is the "finding" of Lady Wisdom (Prov 8:35). Both are gifts of divine favor. They bring life, not death.

3. The word for "watches" or "looks to" in Prov 31:27 is rendered in Hebrew *sopiyya. The New Jerome Bible Commentary,* Prentice Hall, 1968, p. 461, makes the point that *sopiyya* "is a hymnic participle and a play on the Greek word for wisdom, *sophia.*" To the very end the connection between the faithful wife and Lady Wisdom has been sustained.

4. "It has been suggested that the 'stranger' is a devotee of the Canaanite fertility cult that seduced so many Israelites" (Roland Murphy in TOL 17).

Chapter 17

1. A sample of this customary form of address occurs in the instructions given by the vizier Ptah-hotep in ANET 412. Cf. also ANET 412–421 and 427–428.

2. Both the number 375 and the poetic parallel form are artificial contrivances designed to give the proverbs a Solomonic ring, even though many of them are cultural imports of another time and place.

Notes

3. Quoted in Carole R. Fontaine, *Traditional Sayings in the Old Testament,* Bible and Literature Series 5, Almond Press, 1982, p. 270

4. Cf. Song of Songs, 2:7, 9, 17.

Bibliography
and abbreviations used in text

The Anchor Bible: Proverbs, Ecclesiastes, vol. 18, Doubleday, 1965. (Abbrev. as AB)

Ancient Near Eastern Texts, ed. James Pritchard, 3d ed., Princeton University Press, 1969. (Abbrev. as ANET)

Collegeville Bible Commentary—Introduction to Wisdom Literature: Proverbs, by Lawrence E. Boadt, C.S.P., vol. 18, Liturgical Press, 1986. (Abbrev. as CBC)

A New Catholic Commentary on Holy Scripture, Reginald C. Fuller, gen. ed.; Leonard Johnston, O.T. ed.; Conleth Kearns, N.T. ed.; Thomas Nelson, 1969. (Abbrev. as CCHS)

Complete Poems of Francis Thompson, Modern Library, 1913 (?) (Abbrev. as CPFT)

The Complete Poetical Works of William Wordsworth, Macmillan, 1928. (Abbrev. as CPWW)

The Complete Writer's Guide: Questions of Language, by A. Franklin Parks and Richard M. Trask, Philosophical Library, 1985.

Bibliography

Discovering Prophecy and Wisdom, by Margaret Nutting Ralph, Paulist Press, 1993.

The Elements of Style, by William Strunk and E. B. White, 3d ed., Macmillan 1979.

Harper Bible Commentary, ed. J. L. Maya, Harper and Row, 1998. (Abbrev. as HBC)

King James Version. (Abbrev. as KJV)

New American Bible, Confraternity of Christian Doctrine, 1970 (the quotations in this book are taken from NAB unless otherwise stated). (Abbrev. as NAB)

Preaching Proverbs, by Alyce M. McKenzie, Westminster Press, 1996.

The Tree of Life, by Roland E. Murphy, 2d ed., William Eerdmans, 1990. (Abbrev. as TOL)

Understanding the Old Testament, by Bernhard W. Anderson, 2d ed., Prentice Hall, 1966. (Abbrev. as UOT)

Who Wrote the Bible? by Richard Elliott Friedman, Harper, 1987. (Abbrev. as WWB)

General Index

General Index

General Index

Index of Biblical Texts Cited

Index of Biblical Texts Cited

Index of Biblical Texts Cited